The first act [in *Shockers Delight!*] is filled with brittle, sophisticated dialogue—in fact some of the best Lemoine has ever penned. . . . For 16 years and an astonishing 36 plays, Lemoine has carried on a love affair with language.

—Colin MacLean, *Edmonton Sun*

"The poignancy of the insight will startle and delight you."

—Liz Nicholls, *Edmonton Journal*

"His plays have a wry self-awareness and *Pith!* isn't merely an agreeable diversion; it's also a jaunty salute to the powers of the imagination and to the joyous game of "let's pretend" that lies at the heart of all theatre."

—*Calgary Herald*

A Teatro Trilogy

A Teatro Trilogy

Selected Plays by
STEWART LEMOINE

 Prairie Play Series: 23 /Series Editor: Diane Bessai

National Library of Canada Cataloguing in Publication
Lemoine, Stewart, 1960-
A Teatro trilogy : selected plays / Stewart Lemoine.

(Prairie play series : 23)
Contents: Shockers delight!—Pith!—The margin of the sky.
ISBN 1-896300-80-4

I. Title. II. Series.

PS8573.E552T42 2004   C812'.54   C2004-900711-4

Editor for the press: Anne Nothof
Cover photo and design: Peter Edwards
Author photo: Jeff Haslam
The interior photos have been produced with the kind permission of the photographers listed below each photo.

Canadian   Patrimoine
Heritage   canadien

THE CANADA COUNCIL | LE CONSEIL DES ARTS
FOR THE ARTS | DU CANADA
SINCE 1957 | DEPUIS 1957

NeWest Press acknowledges the support of the Canada Council for the Arts, The Alberta Foundation for the Arts, and the Edmonton Arts Council for our publishing program. We also acknowledge the financial support of the Government of Canada through the Book Publishing Industry Development Program (BPIDP) for our publishing activities.

NeWest Press
201-8540-109 Street
Edmonton, Alberta
T6G 1E6
T: (780) 432-9427
F: (780) 433-3179
www.newestpress.com

1 2 3 4 5 08 07 06 05 04

PRINTED AND BOUND IN CANADA

I was recapturing the spirit of play—not the play of youth which is games (aggression under the restraint of rules), but the play of childhood which is all imagination, which improvises. I became light-headed. The spirit of play swept away the cynicism and indifference into which I had fallen. Moreover, a readiness for adventure reawoke in me—for risk, for intruding myself into the lives of others, for extracting fun from danger.

—*Thornton Wilder*
Theophilous North

Contents

Stewart Lemoine's Canadian Comedia

For more than twenty years, Edmonton playwright Stewart Lemoine has investigated the complexities of human relationships and behaviour through witty philosophical paradoxes and ironic observation. His plays comprise a Canadian Comedy of Manners, integrating the popular culture of film and television with the aesthetics of music, design, and theatre. As *The Edmonton Journal* theatre reviewer, Liz Nicholls has observed:

> Stewart Lemoine has always been attracted by the interplay of innocence and worldliness, the exotic and the matter-of-fact. His characters take extravagant philosophical positions on things like hair or Hungarian goulash (Aug 14, 1994).

Lemoine co-wrote his first play, *All These Heels*, for the Edmonton Fringe Festival in 1982. Over the next two decades, he has provided a new play (sometimes two) for nearly every annual Fringe, always using it as an opportunity for experiment with extravagantly imaginative premises, eccentric characters, and exotic locales. Audiences have always expected substantial productions, despite the minimal resources. In *Cocktails at Pams*, for example, first produced in 1986 and revived at five year intervals ever since, eleven actors attended an on-stage cocktail party in real time. In *The Swift Hotel* (1990), seventeen actors created a day in the life of an Argentine hotel in 1950. *Two Tall, Too Thin* (1992) was set on a Malibu terrace with a whole complement of barware, and required seven costume changes for the leading lady—"all intensely glamorous." Audiences often wondered whether Broadway had relocated to the Fringe. But the main impetus of a Lemoine comedy is the language and the characters, not the production values. Lemoine ended his association with the Fringe in 2003, preferring to focus his attention on developing a season of plays for his company, Teatro La Quindicina. They had reached a point where they needed to solidify their main season activities at the Varscona Theatre, where they have developed a loyal and large audience beyond the parameters of the Fringe.

Teatro La Quindicina has been in an ongoing process of development ever since its inception at the first Fringe in 1982. The name is serendipitous: someone happened to be reading Graham Greene's *Travels with My Aunt* at the time. In her colourful but shady past, the aunt had travelled with a high-class bordello called "La Quindicina," the Italian word for "fifteen," referring to the group's bi-monthly itinerary. "La Quindicina" was often mistaken for a theatre company. Lemoine's company confirmed the association by adding "Teatro" to "La Quindicina," and used it on the Fringe application form. When the Fringe returned the following summer, they used the same name to announce their continuing existence. Teatro La Quindicina has been resident in the Varscona Theatre in Old Strathcona, Edmonton since 1994

The company comprises a core group of Edmonton actors who have a long-term relationship with Lemoine and his plays. The actors who created roles in this collection all have strong ties to the company. Leona Brausen was part of Teatro's inception in 1982, Davina Stewart joined in 1986, Jeff Haslam and Cathy Derkach in 1988, and Julien Arnold in 1990. Ron Pederson debuted in 1992 at the age of fifteen as a member of Teatro Bambino, a company of teens who created Fringe productions under Lemoine's guidance. Julien Arnold, Leona Brausen, Jeff Haslam, Davina Stewart, and Sheri Somerville are also designated artistic associates of Teatro, assisting with its operations and long-term planning, and Brausen often designs the costumes for the productions. Depending on the requirements of each play, the company is expanded to include other actors from the Edmonton community and occasionally further afield. Frequent Teatro performers include Andrea House, John Kirkpatrick, Cathleen Rootsaert, Kate Ryan, Jane Spidell, and Barbara Gates Wilson, as well as such emerging artists as Joceyln Ahlf, Briana Buckmaster, Josh Dean, and Celina Stachow. As Lemoine has explained, he wants to know what the people he writes for are like, before he subverts them, and he does not remount his plays until he has found the right combination of actors.

According to Lemoine, there is a sense of mutual loyalty in Teatro, a feeling of like-mindedness and trust. The company spends a lot of time in rehearsal yakking. Everyone thinks at the same level and with the same intensity. Lemoine believes that "people come to the plays because they like the actors as much as they like the writing." He specifically writes his plays for members of the company, although he also exercises his freedom to diversify the cast, depending on the requirements of the plays, and the availability of the actors. He plays on their strengths, and what he thinks they can do. Given the challenge of creating a three-hander for women, he wrote *When Girls Collide*, an all-girl "film noir." Knowing who was in the cast, and what kinds of characters were particular to the genre, he could envision specific individuals: an authoritative mystery "woman in black;" a vivaciously "trashy blonde;" an addled housewife turned detective.

Teatro La Quindicina has produced the works of other playwrights; for example *Rope* by Patrick Hamilton, a metaphysical mystery from the 1920s for the 1993 Fringe; *Anatol* by Arthur Schnitzler; and *Hedda Gabler* by Henrik Ibsen, which provided a challenging vehicle for Davina Stewart. Lemoine prefers to produce and direct his own plays, however. He knows his audience and what to do for them. He has experimented with other styles—the expressionism of Judith Thompson in *Neck-Breaking Car-Hop*, and the psychological intensity of Ibsen, Strindberg, and Wedekind in *The Vile Governess*—but there is always a comic spin that is distinctively his.

Typically Lemoine's plays feature bizarre scenarios, witty dialogue, and quirky characters, whether they were written specifically for the Fringe or not. Some, like the plays in this collection, are more reflective, more philosophical; others are what Lemoine terms his "Screwball Comedies," such as *On the Banks of the Nut*, *Vidalia*, and *Skirts on Fire*, which was revived for the 2003/04 Teatro season. Lemoine describes his "Screwball Comedies" as "fast-paced, intricately plotted, and peopled by characters who retain a literate air even under the absurd amounts of pressure." In her preview of *Skirts on Fire* in *The Edmonton Journal*, Liz Nicholls celebrates Lemoine as "Canada's King of the Screwball": his plays are acts of "almost willful eccentricity." In a "moody era," in which comedies "can't hold their heads up in public without a dark, morbid streak [and] '[f]unny' is some sort of defensive position . . . in an age when no self-respecting comedy can afford to be angst-free, what do you make of a frothy form where people blithely meddle in each other's affairs, complicate them for the sheer pleasure of making life more and more interesting?" (Nov 6, 2003)

Lemoine believes that even in the most grim circumstances there may be humour. Someone always has some darkly comic comment to make. Too many contemporary tragedies are completely bleak. The audience understands the message and sees the importance of it, but they are glad when the play is over. Lemoine prefers to keep his works engaging and humorous at many levels—side-splitting or whimsical. In *Shockers Delight!*, for example, although two of the characters are given to wisecracks and jokes to evade important issues, they have to adjust to a more serious level.

Most of Lemoine's plays are set in the past, often in the 1940s and '50s. He grew up watching old movies on TV, and his plays are informed by film and television, as much as by literature and theatre. He is cognizant of what people want to see when they go to the theatre, and this may not necessarily be contemporary situations. Much can be said about the present day and the unchanging aspects of people by showing them in past contexts—like the reverse of Shakespeare in modern dress. The use of a traditional genre can provide a certain distance for the observation of human foibles. According to Lemoine, it's also a way of reminding people that this is one way that they can be, whereas if a play is set in the present, the implication is that this is how people all are. Moreover, it can be exciting just to see a period genre recreated live—"film noir" in *When Girls Collide*, or gothic romance inspired by Anne Radcliffe in *The Spanish Abbess of Pilsen*. Lemoine's advice to his audience is uncomplicated: "Just watch these people. They are going to enact a story for you, and you can take whatever you want from it. You can say, 'How did they ever walk in those shoes?' Or 'What was it like back then?' In the 1950s era of *Shockers Delight!*, for example, it was racy to go on a date in a boat and drink, whereas now it looks quaint, so there's some kind of authenticity, as well as period charm."

Lemoine's plays have a distinctly philosophical bent—how to recognize the choices, how to achieve a balance between what appear to be different or conflicting values. There is often a reconciliation at the end, a recognition of integrity and honesty. Marcus in *Shockers Delight!*—like the wise fool in Shakespeare's plays—appreciates the value of using time wisely, and the infinite possibilities which may lie ahead. In his last speech, floating on a lake in boat, suspended in time, he experiences a moment when he lives in harmony with himself, his friends, and his environment. Lemoine's plays are inquiries into the nature of friendship and love, finding that they are very much the same, but for particular circumstances—and that logic and reason are ineffectual in matters of the heart. There is some sadness in this realization, but also some happiness in the recognition of the power of these feelings, and how they can change lives. Not to admit the importance of these feelings can result in disaster, as Marcus discovers in *Shockers Delight!*

In all of Lemoine's plays, the creative imagination is a means by which fantasies become psychological realities, often transforming lives and offering the possibility of hope and redemption. As he has pointed out in respect to the three plays in this collection:

> All feature sequences that are the product of the characters' imaginations. In *The Margin of the Sky* the bulk of the play turns out to have been Leo's idealized version of a day he'd rather be having. In *Shockers Delight!* the Biedermeier game-playing is where Marcus finds equilibrium and refuge from illness and unhappiness. In *Pith!* Virginia is taken on a fantastic imaginary journey as a means of dealing with an overwhelming emotional obstacle. I think that in all three there's a kind of eventual transcendence where the characters come to realize the difference between what is real and what isn't and gain a kind of enduring strength from it.

In *Pith!* the imaginary journey from a manor in Rhode Island to a hotel in New Orleans and the jungles of Panama and Ecuador, during which a grieving, closeted widow and her intrepid Nancy Drew sidekick meet an assortment of strange and exotic strangers, is accomplished on a bare stage with four chairs and a Victrola, testifying to the powerful illusions of theatre. And the master manipulator of illusions, the mysterious sailor, Jack Vail, plays many roles as he guides the two women through dangerous adventures to a more positive future. Equatorial nights might be variable in duration, but the sun always comes up.

All three plays respond to the question: "Well . . . what if THIS happened?" But there is also a grounding in reality, often in the casual incidents of the playwright's life. Lemoine's experiences in the United States anticipate Leo's in *The Margin of the Sky*—being asked for assistance by another customer at Tower Records in New York; being bemused by the surreal, frenetic, cool ambiance of Los Angeles while not quite connecting with an actress over a script-writing opportunity.

Lemoine locates his ingenuous characters in the United States or in exotic foreign locales to show their response to seductive but dangerous social and cultural systems, and to explore their potential for independent self-realization. In *The Margin of the Sky* he places the different cultural perspectives in the United States and Canada in ironic juxtaposition. Leo, the quintessential Canadian playwright, with the propensity to see irony in everything, finds he cannot accommodate the melodramatic and violent scenarios required by Hollywood. But he can appreciate the infinite possibilities of the imagination and the human heart—in a sunset, in music.

The titles of Lemoine's plays are always unusual and quizzical. Many prompt an excursion to the dictionary or encyclopedia, although others are simply taken from the vocabulary of Lemoine's personal experience. The exclamatory phrase, *Shockers Delight!* was concocted by a high school friend. It just means "Holy Toot!"—an expression of amazement. It's also an oxymoron that underscores the paradoxes in the play—the shock of being hit on the head that has surprising consequences. *Pith!* suggests the lightweight helmet affected by African adventurers, but it also has the denotation of "quintessence" or "the essential part"—as in the *pith* of an argument, or "physical strength and vigour." According to Lemoine, following the production of the play, there was a spike in the usage of "pith" in Edmonton conversations.

The title *The Margin of the Sky* is taken from an English translation of the words of Danish poet Jens Peter Jacobsen for the first aria in *Gurrelieder*, a massive cantata by Austrian composer Arnold Schoenberg (1874-1951). This aria is sung by the doomed hero, Waldemar as he rides to meet his loved one, Tove, whom he has established in the castle of Gurre:

> Now dusk mutes every sound
> on land and sea.
> the scudding clouds have gathered close
> against the margin of the sky.

Tove is murdered by Waldemar's jealous queen, and the anguished Waldemar curses God, for which he is condemned after his death to rise from his grave and ride with his followers every night.

Schoenberg completed *Gurrelieder* in 1901, although it was not performed until 1913. It is an enormous three-part work, combining elements of song cycle, oratorio, melodrama, opera, and symphony, written in the late romantic style of Mahler and Wagner. But it is also moving towards the atonalism which Schoenberg developed in his later works, taking the "left turn" or intellectual risk that Leo urges of his new friends in Lemoine's play. In performance it requires over four-hundred musicians, including five solo singers, a speaker, three-part male choruses, eight-part mixed choir, and a large orchestra. As Spence, the soap opera star in *The Margin of the Sky* comments, it can be overwhelmingly "loud," but it begins with a quiet evocation of forest birds and of the setting sun—like Lemoine's play. Following the production of *The Margin of the Sky*, there was a spike in purchases of *Gurrelieder* at The Gramophone in Edmonton.

In Lemoine's play, passages from *Gurrelieder* transpose the characters from real to imagined space. As they regard the setting sun through dark glasses in the patio scene, Spence, Alice, and Sheila speculate on the meaning of "the margin of the sky." Leo, however, protests that he "doesn't know what [they] want to know, and [he] doesn't know why [he's] supposed to know it." When he returns to reality in his office, and informs Spence that he will not write his film script, Leo again immerses himself in the imagined world of

Schoenberg's opera, and notices "something extremely obvious on his notepad." He can now offer an interpretation to his imagined friends in a speech that *See* reviewer Gilbert A. Bouchard terms "a real tour-de-force that makes semiotic ramble sing sweetly" (www.seemagazine.com, May 29, 2003). An end can become a beginning:

A margin is an edge. And on a piece of paper, it's a line that marks an edge, but it really only has meaning because it denotes a point of entry. You put your pen where the margin tells you to and that's it . . . You're in. So the margin of the sky would have to be the point of entry for everything above. That's why you can never say it's the least significant part . . . The sky is huge. You can't pick a place to get into it just by looking up. But if you look straight on . . . you can let yourself think that there really is a part of the sky that touches this same earth on which we're all standing.

You can let yourself think that if you traveled the distance between here and there you would actually get to it.

Leo, the Canadian playwright, finds a way of entering an imagined space through language. To quote Homi Bhabha (citing Heidegger), "a boundary is not just a line at which something stops but a line from which something begins its presencing." Margins, like borders and boundaries, give rise to alternative sites of meaning.

Music is a prominent feature in many of Lemoine's plays. It creates the possibility of transformation. In *The Margin of the Sky*, as Liz Nicholls points out in her review of the play, "*Gurrelieder* is a trigger for all revelations and self-discoveries tumbling through the play" (May 24, 2003). In *Shockers Delight!* Schubert's piano music accompanies Marcus as he philosophizes in his boat, pointing to "something deeply melancholy in this portrait of friends too bright not to comprehend life's possibilities" (Nicholls, Feb 14, 1993). In *Pith!*, the widow Mrs. Virginia Tilford, obsessively plays darkly melancholy arias sung by Rosa Ponselle (1897-1981), a Metropolitan opera star discovered by Enrico Caruso. For Lemoine, music is inspirational, evocative, informative. It underscores his words, images, and characters.

Shockers Delight! is informed by another of Lemoine's unusual analogies—Biedermeier—an aesthetic style and social philosophy which prevailed in Germany and Austria in the first half of the nineteenth century following the French Revolution and Napoleonic wars, and enjoyed a revival in the 1950s when the play is set. It was a scaling down and simplification of design, architecture, and life— a rebellion against the excesses of the Baroque period which preceded it. In respect to furniture design, it produced functional pieces with slim straight legs and even surfaces that fit neatly into homes—an attempt to follow nature by using natural woods free of ornamentation. Its sensibilities were bourgeois, like those of the 1950s following the Second World War, and the prevailing attitude was that it was time to be at home, to make the garden grow, and to raise the family. In *Shockers Delight!* Marcus proclaims Biedermeirer as his philosophy of life, and it eventually provides him with a fantasy that enables him to write a fascinating diary and have many important insights. His friends in effect create through playacting a time and place in which his imagination can flourish.

In *Shockers Delight!* Lemoine also uses dance and golf as ways of exploring a philosophy of life, or a way of living—detecting and sharing impulses and rhythms, while maintaining poise and grace in dance; finding the right stance and grip to achieve a goal in golf. His plays explore ways of achieving balance in a precarious world— through humour, imagination, loyalty, and friendship.

Anne Nothof
Athabasca University
January, 2004

Davina Stewart as Julia, Julien Arnold (kneeling) as Marcus, and Jeff Haslam as Rory in the Teatro La Quindicina production of Shockers Delight!, *Edmonton, Alberta, 1993.*

Photo: Carol Woo

Shockers Delight!

Production History

Shockers Delight! was first produced at the Phoenix Downtown in Edmonton by Teatro La Quindicina, February 1993. The production was remounted by Teatro at Factory Theatre in Toronto, October 1993. It was taped for *Theatre of the Air* on CKUA radio in March, 1993.

A new Teatro production of the play opens at the Varscona Theatre in Edmonton in July, 2004.

C A S T (1993)

Julia Goode	*Davina Stewart*
Marcus Whitelaw	*Julien Arnold*
Rory Stanhope	*Jeff Haslam*

Director	*Stewart Lemoine*
Set and Lighting Designer	*Roger Schultz*
Costume Designer	*Melinda Sutton*
Stage Manager (Edmonton)	*Jim Cej*
Stage Manager (Toronto)	*Katherine Ensslen*

C A S T (2004)

Julia Goode	*Jocelyn Ahlf*
Marcus Whitelaw	*Ron Pederson*
Rory Stanhope	*Josh Dean*

Production Notes

Julia Goode
Marcus Whitelaw
Rory Stanhope

When first introduced, all three of these characters are on the verge of completing their first undergraduate degrees, which makes them twenty-one or twenty-two years of age in Act One, and twenty-seven or twenty-eight in Act Two.

SETTING

The University of Continental North America in 1956 (Act One), and in 1962 (Act Two).

The University of Continental North America is conceived as an Ivy League School of the most classic sort. Roger Schultz's set for the Teatro premiere was a large painted backdrop of an imposing vine-covered college building, before which the various scenes were played with minimal additions of furniture and props.

NOTE

A key element in setting the tone of a production of *Shockers Delight!* is the use throughout of Schubert's piano music, which underscores certain moments and plays in all of the scene transitions. Of particular importance are the Impromptu #2 D.935, Op.142, underscoring the opening moments of the play and the last paragraph of Marcus's final speech, and the Impromptu #3 D.899, Op.90 which is played for the transition from Julia alone at the end of Act Two, Scene Three, to Rory alone at the beginning of Act Two, Scene Four. The jolly Biedermeier Dance in Act Two is performed to the "Champagner-Galopp" by Johann Strauss Sr. in a string quartet arrangement played by the Ensemble Biedermeier Wien. The scene which follows is quietly underscored by Joseph Lanner's "Neue Wiener Landler," performed by the same group.

ACT ONE

Scene One

A spring day in 1956. Marcus Whitelaw and Julia Goode are lying on a picnic blanket with a number of books spread out around them. Marcus is reading and making occasional notes. Julia is staring at a book.

Julia: Biedermeier. Biedermeier? Biedermeier . . .

Marcus: What about it?

Julia: Do you know what it is?

Marcus: Furniture. Of a particular kind.

Julia: So the Biedermeier Era would be . . .

Marcus: When they made all the furniture. It was the early nineteenth century, specifically in Germany and Austria.

Julia: That's it. That took a whole era?

Marcus: I think so, post-French Revolution, nothing much doing. Europeans were lying low, staying home . . .

Julia: Making furniture . . .

Marcus: With slim straight legs . . .

Julia: Nothing too ornate . . .

Marcus: Simple, functional . . . bourgeois . . . the new order . . .

Julia: I see it so clearly. Women with tufty hair and puffy sleeves . . .

Marcus: Men with smart vests and curious sideburns . . .

Julia: It's like a Jane Austen world, only everyone has a beer.

Both: Biedermeier.

Marcus:	So what about it?
Julia:	I'm doing a research paper on the origins of the waltz. Biedermeier comes up a lot.
Marcus:	Did they waltz then?
Julia:	They did something like it. They clung to each other and twirled around in three-quarter time.
Marcus:	That's pretty much it then, isn't it?
Julia:	Not entirely. They also slapped their thighs. Somewhere along the line this was dropped. If I could find out when and why, my paper would have substance and application. *She shuts her book.* Though I don't actually give two hoots.
Marcus:	Hoot-hoot.
Julia:	Nope. How come you're so up on Biedermeier?
Marcus:	It was one of my electives last term. I had four months of it.
Julia:	You never mentioned it.
Marcus:	I did too. But you'd always start to nod off.
Julia:	I guess I didn't realize it was fascinating. What are you reading now?
Marcus:	Ovid. He checks the spine. Oh, sorry . . . Plutarch. Guess I better go over some of this again.
Julia:	I have to say Marcus, I'm concerned about our ability to function outside the academic world. We're graduating in a few weeks, and then what will we do?
Marcus:	Julia, I think your education has been pretty career-specific. Your major is ballroom dance.

Julia:	Well maybe it's just your ability to function that worries me. Your major is philosophy, your minor is history. You're twenty-one years old. Marcus, I think you're gonna die.
Marcus:	I've been giving this some thought as well. In the absence of any constructive plan, I think the best thing for me to do is accumulate more degrees.
Julia:	How many?
Marcus:	Three, seven . . . maybe more. I'll just go on till it makes sense, or until I'm crushed by the weight of all that I know.
Julia:	So you really have no plans for the future?
Marcus:	None whatsoever.
Julia:	Well that a relief. I thought that somehow, after all these years, we might have accidentally turned out . . . different.
Marcus:	From each other? Nah.
Julia:	Marcus . . . I have a question.
Marcus:	Julia . . . what is it?
Julia:	I'm wondering . . . Since I'm almost going to be a college graduate—
Marcus:	I think you actually will be one.
Julia:	Fuss fuss fuss. Since I'm about to become a college graduate . . .
Marcus:	Yes?
Julia:	Should I be looking for someone to marry?
Marcus:	I guess it depends.

Julia:	What on?
Marcus:	On whether you want to be married. Do you?
Julia:	I'm sure I would if I met the right sort of man.
Marcus:	And what sort would that be?
Julia:	I suppose . . . someone who wanted to marry me.
Marcus:	Is that all?
Julia:	I'm sure he'd have to have other fine qualities, but that would be the most important of them. So . . . what's the answer?
Marcus:	What was the question again, exactly?
Julia:	Should I be looking for someone to marry?

Pause.

Marcus:	I dunno.
Julia:	Take a stab.
Marcus:	Alright. Sure, look for a husband. Or a job.
Julia:	I'd hoped you'd be more helpful.
Marcus:	I really should be studying philosophy right now.
Julia:	But my questions are of a philosophical nature.
Marcus:	I haven't passed my examinations. I'm not qualified to be of help.
Julia:	Would you ever want to marry me?
Marcus:	I don't think so.
Julia:	Why not?

Marcus: I've known you too long. We've been friends since we were five.

Julia: That's a positive sign, isn't it? I don't really have any friends other than you. Not close ones. So it seems that—

Marcus: Julia, if we were to marry I'd be your husband and you'd have no friends left at all.

Julia: Well, who will I marry then?

Marcus: I don't know. How about that fellow over there. *He waves.* Excuse me!

Julia: Marcus!

Marcus: Hallo! Yes, you . . . Can you come over here a moment?

Julia: Marcus, what are you doing?

Rory enters.

Rory: Are you waving at me?

Marcus: Yes I am. My friend has a question for you.

Rory: Oh? Yes?

Marcus: Go ahead Julia. Ask . . . Sorry, what's your name?

Rory: Rory. Rory Stanhope.

Marcus: Ask Rory your question.

Julia: Which one?

Marcus: The one you asked me.

Julia: Oh . . . well, Rory . . . should I be looking for someone to marry?

Rory: I really have no idea.

Marcus: That's the wrong question Julia.

Julia: Well what . . .

Marcus whispers in her ear.

Julia: I can't ask him that.

Marcus: Fine. Then face the consequences.

Julia looks puzzled, then turns abruptly to Rory.

Julia: Rory, would you ever want to marry me?

Rory: Would I . . . I really have no idea.

Marcus: There isn't actually a correct answer. Keep that in mind.

Julia: But you have no basis for saying no.

Rory: I don't?

Julia: You don't know me well enough to reject me.

Rory: Well then . . . Yes?

Julia: Yes?

Rory: Yes, I might want to marry you. Someday.

Julia: When?

Marcus: I don't think that's a fair question.

Rory: You know, I might also want a divorce.

Marcus: Some other day.

Julia: Please Rory, let's not get ahead of ourselves.

Rory: No, of course not. I beg your pardon Miss . . .

Julia: Goode. Julia. With an E. I mean that's Goode with E.

Rory: Uh-huh. Can I go now? Is this it?

Julia: I think so. Thank you Rory.

Rory: Sure. Bye.

He starts to go.

Marcus: Don't let him go. He wants to marry you.

Julia: He doesn't. Not yet.

Marcus: Nonetheless, what if it's your one chance at happiness? What if you're blowing it here and now? What if you pay for this with sixty years of misery and regret? What if—

Julia: RORY!!

Rory: *Re-enters.* Yes? What?

Marcus: Julia has one more question for you.

Rory: Sure. What's that?

Julia: *Puts her face in her hands.* I forget.

Rory: Oh?

Julia: *Speaking quickly.* Would you mind rowing me across the lake next Sunday afternoon?

Rory: No, I suppose I wouldn't mind. Is this hypothetical too?

Julia: No Rory, I really want to go.

Rory: Well alright. We won't have to get married, will we?

Julia: No, of course not. Oh. That was a joke.

Rory: Well . . . Yeah, sure it was. I'll see you Sunday then . . . at three?

Julia: At three. By the shore?

Rory: By the shore. *Pointing.* There?

Julia: Yes, perfect. Oh . . . You'll have to have a boat.

Rory: A boat? Well yes, I guess I will.

Julia: Goodbye.

Rory exits. Julia watches him go, then sits back on the blanket.

Marcus: Well, you must be excited.

Julia: I'm not sure. I don't think I like boating very much.

Marcus: It's a small down-payment to make for a lifetime of wedded bliss.

Julia: I wonder what you've just done for me.

Marcus: I've complicated your life and by extension, my own.

Julia: Yours? How so?

Marcus: I was lying earlier. I love you madly and want desperately to be your husband.

Julia: It's too late.

Marcus: I hardly think that's true.

Julia: Well then, what are you going to do?

Marcus: I suppose . . . I'll seethe.

He goes back to reading. She watches him. He looks up briefly.

Marcus: Later.

Scene Two

Julia and Rory are in a rowboat in the middle of a lake. Rory rows for a bit, then stops and looks around.

Rory: It's peaceful here, isn't it.

Julia: What, here in the middle of the lake?

Rory: Yeah. It's so calm.

Julia: You really think so?

Rory: Why yes. Don't you?

Julia: Mercy no. The water laps restlessly, even when there's no wind. We rock from side to side, with only a few planks of wood between us and what appears to be deep deep water. This is a completely unnatural place for us to be. Rory, I'm afraid I really can't find much peace in the middle of a lake.

Rory: Well it's quiet at any rate.

Julia: Because everything is so far away. There's no accomplishment in this silence.

Rory: Should I just keep going then? Toward the other side?

Julia: No rush. There's just a big field with nothing to do in it, so we'd have to turn around and come back.

Rory: But if you're not happy here—

Julia: I didn't say I wasn't happy. I'm just not at peace. I wouldn't be at peace no matter where we were.

Rory: No?

Julia: Well no Rory, not on a first date.

Rory: Of course. I'm a little nervous too.

Julia: Well good. *Pause.* Why?

Rory shrugs.

Julia: I don't suppose you brought any whisky and crackers.

Rory: Uh . . . No . . .

Julia: Well I did. *She takes a small flask and a box of crackers from a big straw bag.* I didn't bring any glasses, as there's really no place to put them down. *She takes a swig from the flask and hands it to him.* Here ya go.

Rory: Thanks. *He swigs and chokes a little.* Oh my.

Julia: It's the good stuff.

Rory: I usually take it with a little water.

Julia: Didn't bring any of that I'm afraid.

Rory: *Eyes the lake a little sadly, then takes another swig.* Maybe I'll have a cracker.

Julia: Have two.
Rory: Thanks. *He takes a bite, then has another swig.* These crackers are fine. They aren't salted.

Julia: *Takes back the flask.* No, not even a little.

Pause.

Rory: Are you impatient with me?

Julia: I don't think so. Well, maybe a little. No more than with most people. Is it important?

Rory: I just don't think we're ever going to be in step. I hate to have to say it, but I'm afraid of you.

Julia: Why?

Rory: I can't seem to please you.

Julia: Why would you want to please me?

Rory: We're on a date. Our first date . . . Isn't it my main objective?

Julia: Are you saying I should be nicer?

Rory: Yes. I don't know. I've no idea why I'm here.

Julia: That's easy. I asked you to come.

Rory: But why did I accept?

Julia: That, Rory, is a question you must ask yourself.

Rory: I have. I've asked myself over and over again . . . Why am I going rowing with this strange . . . I mean unknown . . . woman?

Julia: Over and over? Like . . . dozens of times?

Rory: Hundreds. I'm sorry.

Julia: So . . . do you always get the same answer? Are there hundreds of different answers? What?

Rory: I think there's no answer at all.

Julia: So it's sort of . . . Why are you here? *She gestures expansively.* Why are any of us here? Mankind . . . Why . . . ?

Rory: Maybe. Maybe this wouldn't be so hard if I were better at thinking. May I have some more whisky?

Julia: Certainly. *She hands him the flask.* What are you studying?

Rory: All sorts of things.

Julia: Me too. What's your major?

Rory:	Golf.
Julia:	Golf? Is that hard?
Rory:	Not really. Not for me. I've got a kind of . . . *Gestures obliquely* . . . a hand-eye-wrist thing. I guess I'm lucky.
Julia:	Is there a future in golf?
Rory:	The future is what we make of it. There's a future in everything.
Julia:	That's worth believing, I guess.
Rory:	What's your major?
Julia:	Dance.
Rory:	Ballet?
Julia:	Ballroom.
Rory:	I didn't know you could major in that.
Julia:	I didn't know you could major in golf.
Rory:	My parents think the University of Continental North America defines the liberal arts a bit too liberally. But they also had the sense to keep me away from political science.
Julia:	I was an anthropology major until one day I was walking down the hall and I heard mambo music coming out of a classroom. I just stopped and stood there with my ten pounds of books and said "What am I thinkin'?"
Rory:	So . . . could you teach me to dance so that anyone would want to be my partner?
Julia:	I'm certain of it. But why would I want to if you're only going to marry me?
Rory:	I . . . I don't know that that's been decided yet.

Julia:	Okay, just checkin'. *She takes a swig of whisky. There's a little pause.* I've never golfed in my life.
Rory:	Is that deliberate?
Julia:	It must be by now. I mean, I'm twenty-two. Nothing's really accidental at this point.
Rory:	Tell me, Julia, who was that fellow you were with on the picnic blanket the other day?
Julia:	That was Marcus. Marcus Whitelaw. He's an old friend.
Rory:	So you're not likely to marry him?
Julia:	I doubt it. I think he's on to me.
Rory:	What do you mean?
Julia:	Tsk. If I told you . . .
Rory:	*Smacks his forehead.* Oh, right . . .
Julia:	Whisky?
Rory:	Thanks.
Julia:	Go ahead and finish it.
Rory:	You sure?
Julia:	Yup.
Rory:	*Takes another swig.* I have to say . . . I'm still not sure that I don't want to marry you.
Julia:	And why do you have to say that?
Rory:	Because it's the one thing that I'm certain of. I mean, I didn't know you well enough to reject you before, and I still don't.
Julia:	So you're just going to have to get to know me better.

Rory:	It seems so. But what if . . . Isn't it possible that it might become even more difficult?
Julia:	What? To reject me?
Rory:	Exactly.
Julia:	Well that's just a great big risk for us Rory.
Rory:	Like sitting in a rowboat.
Julia:	Floating over unfathomable depths.
Rory:	*Takes a swig, then holds the flask upside down.* Uh-oh.
Julia:	You've taken me at my word.
Rory:	Was that wrong of me?
Julia:	In this case, no. *She reaches into the bottle and pulls out a large bottle of whisky.* For I've another bottle, larger than the last.
Rory:	*Looks at the flask.* But why . . . ?
Julia:	First impressions . . . etcetera. *She takes a big swig and hands him the bottle.*
Rory:	I don't suppose you actually do have glasses in there.
Julia:	There are some things about me you're going to just have to accept.
Rory:	Sure.

He takes a big swig, followed by another. He offers her the bottle and she declines. He puts it down. They stare at each other, smiling, but not inclined to speak.

Rory:	So . . .
Julia:	So?

Rory: What?

Julia: I don't know.

Rory: *Holds up the box.* Cracker?

Julia: No. I—

She lunges forward suddenly, and they heave from side to side, trying desperately to retain balance. They finally steady themselves so that he's lying back and she's perched overtop of him.

Rory: What exactly are you trying to do?

Julia: I was lunging. I wanted to kiss you. On the mouth.

Rory: Oh. That's not fair.

Julia: It isn't?

Rory: I was just thinking of lunging at you. Now I can't, really.

Julia: Mmm. Tough.

They kiss. Julia pulls away after a bit.

Rory: Wow.

Julia: Exactly. *She sits back and picks up her bag.* Would you like a boilermaker?

Rory: I beg your pardon?

Julia: I brought a couple of bottles of beer . . . *She produces these* . . . and an opener.

Rory: But don't you need big tumblers? And a shot glass. You definitely need a shot glass.

Julia: Listen to you. A shot glass . . . You're like a girl on a camping trip, aren't ya? A shot glass? You just . . .

She holds a beer bottle and the whisky bottle to her mouth and guzzles from them simultaneously. She lowers them, gargles, swallows, then dabs her mouth with her sleeve.

Julia: See.

Rory: Got it.

He lifts the bottles to his mouth, then thinks better of it. He leans over the edge of the boat, then drinks. When he's done, he gives the bottles back to Julia.

Rory: There. And no mess in the boat.

Julia: Smartie. *She leans over the side and drinks. She sets the bottles down and looks pointedly at Rory.* Your turn.

Rory: What?

Julia: To lunge.

Rory: But it won't be a surprise. It's no fun if it's not a surprise.

Julia: Are you insane?

Rory: What?

Julia: How can you say it wou—

He lunges over her and they steady themselves for a moment.

Julia: Maybe we ought to be careful about tipping the boat. I don't recall being able to swim.

Rory: I'll save you. And I think it's not actually that deep here.

Julia: You can drown in a bathtub Rory.

Rory: But you never do.

Julia: You're right. What a wonderful thing. Nonetheless . . .

Rory: Uh-huh?

Julia: Don't ever move again.

Rory: Okay.

They kiss.

Scene Three
On the University grounds. Marcus enters, skipping rope.

Marcus: Million five, million six, million seven, million eight . . .

Julia enters behind Marcus and watches him. Still skipping and counting, he gradually turns around and sees her. He continues to skip through their conversation.

Marcus: Good morning Julia.

Julia: Good morning.

Marcus: So, how was your date?

Julia: Fine.

Marcus: Fine? That's all.

Julia: Well, more than that. It was . . . Can you stop skipping for a moment?

Marcus: I really shouldn't. I've got to do at least fifty thousand more.

Julia: Well it's irritating and I'm just going to go.

Marcus: *Stops.* Fine then. I'll stop for a bit.

Julia: What are you trying to achieve anyway?

Marcus: It's good for the calves. Here, feel . . .

Julia:	Don't be disgusting.
Marcus:	No really, just touch . . . *He takes her hand and makes her prod his calf.*
Julia:	Hm . . . Wearing high heels would give the same result.
Marcus:	People would judge me unfairly.
Julia:	Well skipping's a pretty woossie pantywaist activity if you ask me.
Marcus:	All the great boxers have skipped.
Julia:	They also boxed.
Marcus:	So tell me about your date. Was it awful? Is that why you're such a miserable pus-hag today?
Julia:	Not a bit of it. I'm just a little hung over.
Marcus:	It was memorable then?
Julia:	What I remember of it certainly was.
Marcus:	And how much of it is that?
Julia:	I think actually . . . everything.
Marcus:	Is he still willing to marry you?
Julia:	Well he's not willing to not marry me.
Marcus:	So things haven't changed?
Julia:	Oh Marcus, no! That's where you're wrong.
Marcus:	He kissed you?
Julia:	Oh yes.
Marcus:	After you kissed him?

Julia:	Well . . . yeah.
Marcus:	Tramp.
Julia:	Am not.
Marcus:	Okay.
Julia:	My intentions are honorable. Marriage is my objective.
Marcus:	Gold-digger.
Julia:	Am not.
Marcus:	Okay. *Pause.* But . . .
Julia:	But what?
Marcus:	I'd really like to know . . . Why marriage? Why are you actually even talking about marriage? Why can't you just go on inconsequential dates and enjoy that?
Julia:	I don't know. A thing worth doing . . .
Marcus:	But don't you think there's a danger that your intensity might limit your prospects?
Julia:	WHY ARE YOU TORTURING ME WITH THESE QUESTIONS????!!!
Marcus:	Well you won't let me skip.
Julia:	Go ahead. Skip.
Marcus:	You can join me if you want.
Julia:	How?
Marcus:	It's easy. We'll just tie one end here . . . *He ties one end of the rope to a railing or some other immovable object.* And I just turn like so . . . *Turns rope.* And you can jump.

Julia: Marcus, I really don't think I'm up to this sort of—

Marcus: I SAID JUMP, WOMAN!!!

Julia leaps into the path of the rope and starts skipping.

Marcus: Hee hee. Are you enjoying yourself?

Julia: What do you think?

Marcus: You're supposed to recite a little rhyme.
Julia: I don't know any.

Marcus: Come on!

Julia: "Milton! Thou shoud'st be living at this hour!"

Marcus: Wrong.

Julia: "Thou still unravished bride of quietness . . ."

Marcus: *Stops turning.* That's not it either.

Julia: Well what then?

Marcus: Julia and Rory, sittin' in a tree . . .

Julia: Try again. It was a boat, not a tree, and . . . Here, I know.

He resumes turning and she skips.

> Now I lay me down to sleep
> I pray the Lord my soul to keep
> If I should die before I wake
> Then you my friend will have more cake. ·

Marcus: You're not finished.

Julia: I am too.

Marcus: You're supposed to say one more thing.

Julia: Amen?

Marcus: Pepper!!

He turns the rope at double speed. Julia shrieks and skips as long as she can before stumbling away laughing.

Marcus: Nyah-nyah-nyah . . .

Julia: Marcus, look at you. You look like you're seven years old.

Marcus: Huh?

Julia: You look exactly like you did when you were seven. You've always looked the same and you always will. I don't think you're ever going to change.

Marcus: I'll take that as a compliment and thank you Julia.

Julia: Do you think I've changed? When I was skipping, did I look like I was seven again?

Marcus: I'd have to say no, not in that sweater.

Julia: *Backs away.* Ooo, that was a dirty thing to say. Marcus Whitelaw, you apologize to me!

Marcus: Don't have to. Just said what I thought on account of what I saw.

Julia: You say you're sorry.

Marcus: I'm not sorry. I'm not, I'm not, I'm not.

Julia: Get off our property!

Marcus: Don't have to!

Julia: My Dad's gonna give you a lickin'!

Marcus: What about your boyfriend? What about big ol' Rory Stanhope? Can't he defend you?

Julia: Marcus!

She punches him hard in the stomach. He doubles over and falls.

Marcus: Ough! Julia!!

Julia: *Steps back.* Oh no . . . Marcus . . . I'm sorry. I'm a little wound up I guess.

Marcus: I guess.

She runs out, leaving Marcus looking rather puzzled.

Scene Four
A dance classroom, late at night. There's a record player and some albums, as well as a flip chart depicting feet in various dance positions. Rory is looking at this as Julia enters.

Rory: Oh! Hi.

Julia: Hi. Glad you could make it.

Rory: Yeah. Yeah.

She advances toward him. They kiss, awkwardly at first, then rather less so, then they break apart.

Julia: Well.

Rory: Well?

Julia: Would you . . . care to dance?

Rory: Now?

Julia: Whenever you're ready.

Rory: I guess I'm ready now. What'll we be doing? Should I warm up? Exercise?

Julia:	Do you normally? When you go dancing?
Rory:	No. I suppose I'd normally get a bit looped first.
Julia:	We're not doing that this time. This is another kind of date. We're going to focus our attention on performing an activity together.
Rory:	I think that's smart. We don't want things to stagnate.
Julia:	Oh boy, no. Not on the second date. So, today's activity will be . . . the merengue. Do you know it?
Rory:	Not by name.
Julia:	It's favourite of mine, a Latin dance with modified hip action and no movement above the waist. The secret of the merengue is in the dragging of the foot. There is a story behind this dance and I will tell it to you, as it is a passionate tale and never fails to move me.

This is the national dance of the Dominican Republic. During one of the many revolutions which have occurred in that unfortunate and volatile country, a great national hero was shot and wounded in the leg. When he returned home to his native village there was a great victory celebration, at which all the dancers were obliged to drag one foot out of sympathy and admiration for this great man. We'll start with a basic Cuban Motion. Do you know it? |
Rory:	Uh . . . Not by name.
Julia:	Watch then. *She demonstrates the Cuban Motion, stepping from side to side and shifting the weight on her hips.* There. Can you do that?
Rory:	I expect so. *He does it with no trouble at all.*
Julia:	Well my goodness. That's just exactly it. Tremendous.

Rory shrugs.

Julia:	Have you had dance lessons before?

Rory: Not really. Just in school, when they teach you the box step and the polka.

Julia: Well let's get right to it then, shall we? We start in a closed position.

They stand face to face, his left hand holding her right, her left hand on his shoulder, his right hand on her shoulder.

Julia: You can put your hand on my waist Rory.

Rory: Sorry.

He puts his hand on her waist.

Julia: But don't wiggle your fingers.

Rory: Sorry.

Julia: Now we're just going to start by doing the Cuban Motion together. Alright?

Rory: Yup.

Julia: Good. And one two three four, one two three four. *They move from side to side, again with no difficulty.* That's great. That's exactly it again. Wow.

Rory shrugs.

Julia: Now we just add a couple of quarter turns. Step step turn together, step step turn together. Fine. And grapevine to the left. Step behind, step cross, step in front, step together.

All this is executed easily.

Julia: I think you've done this before.

Rory: I may have. It's not like I've never been to a dance.

Julia: But these steps are complicated.

Rory: Sure, I guess they are.

Julia: But you just do them.

Rory: Well how hard is it supposed to be?

Julia: This is my major. I'm supposed to be much better at it than you.

Rory: I'll bet you understand the philosophy of it better than I do.

Julia: But I could explain that and then you'd know it too. I'm really questioning the point of my education at this moment.

Rory: Was it that you wanted to be superior at something?

Julia: Well yes. I mean . . . no. That'd be reprehensible. Ha ha. Let's just dance.

Rory: I don't mind.

Julia switches on the record player and puts down the needle. Merengue music is heard.

Julia: Ahh, the seductive rhythm of the merengue. Like a tropical breeze it warms us. our hearts beat in two four time, syncopated in every other measure. Our hips—

Rory: Our hips tingle!

Julia: Wow! Merengue!

They latch onto one another and merengue with finesse. Initially they dance without speaking, but as the dance progresses they begin to converse.

Julia: I have to say, this is truly an unexpected pleasure.

Rory: I suppose I have to agree.

Julia: But it's not a complete surprise?

Rory: Oh definitely it is. I thought we were just going to neck.

Julia: What insane presumption!

Rory: You just said to meet you in at midnight in a deserted classroom. I don't know, I just thought . . .

Julia: I hope you're not disappointed.

Rory: Not at all. I'm just wondering what'll happen when the music ends.

Julia: Wait and see I guess.

Rory: That's not like you.

Julia: You think I'm fast, don't you?

Rory: I was going to say lively.

Julia: Not lovely?

Rory: That too. *He dips her.*

Julia: Hey, no! We don't dip in the merengue.

Rory: If you say so.

Julia: I do and you'd better respect it.

Rory: I apologize. Humbly.

Julia: Marvelous. Oh-oh.

Rory: What?

Julia: I think this is the end.

Rory: You might be right.

They end with a little flourish as the music runs out, then find themselves staring into each other's eyes.

Rory: Is there anything on the flip side.

Julia: I think it's the Peabody? Know it?

Rory: Not by name, but probably.

Julia: Then there's not much point in teaching it to you.

Rory: Probably not.

They kiss lingeringly, then break apart slowly.

Rory: You know Julia, if we were to go on another date, and I'm not saying that we necessarily will, even though you are lively . . . I think we could see how you'd do on the golf course.

Julia: You mean playing golf?

Rory: I . . . Yes! I meant playing golf.

Julia: Then I think it's out of the question.

Rory: Why?

Julia: What if I were to excel, just as you've done tonight?

Rory: Well . . . wouldn't that be . . . swell?

Julia: Oh no. Ballroom dancing is collaborative by nature. Golf, as I understand it, is competitive. Whenever we played together, one of us would have to win. That would eat away at the fabric of our relationship. It'd jeopardize our chances of having a happy marriage.

Rory: So we're back to that are we?

Julia: I'm sorry, but yes, I guess we are. Do you think my single-mindedness limits my prospects?

Rory: Uh, not really. It makes me fairly certain of what mine are.

Julia: It does? *She gasps.* Rory Stanhope! That was crass! I oughta slap your face!

Rory: No, don't.

Julia: Okay.

They kiss.

Scene Five
Marcus reclines on a blanket with books, as before. Julia wanders on.

Julia: Marcus.

Marcus: Julia.

Julia: You're studying.

Marcus: Yup.

Julia: Marcus, I'm engaged.

Marcus: Shutup, you are not.

Julia: But I am.

Marcus: To the golfer?

Julia: To Rory Stanhope.

Marcus: After how many dates?

Julia: Five. Five and a half? But by the time we're married, we'll have been on five or six more, so it's not really as reckless as all that. We're going to elope after commencement.

Marcus: Aren't you going to tell your family?

Julia: Eventually. My mother would just want it all done up big and we'd end up having to put it off.

Marcus:	At least another three weeks.
Julia:	Well that would be unbearable.
Marcus:	Puh.
Julia:	Why don't you just offer your opinion Marcus?
Marcus:	Alright. I think you have a malfunction of the brain. Someday you'll look back on this decision and you'll laugh. Then you'll put a bullet through your own head.
Julia:	You don't like Rory, do you?
Marcus:	I don't know him. You don't either.
Julia:	Do too.
Marcus:	Do— *He covers his mouth and looks away.*
Julia:	I know him better than you do, and I don't think you ought to presume to judge him.
Marcus:	But I can judge you.
Julia:	I wish you wouldn't.
Marcus:	Then you shouldn't have asked my opinion.
Julia:	This was all your idea. You set us up, practically.
Marcus:	Fine then. I wish you every happiness.
Julia:	Marcus, this might seem like a strange request, but will you give me away?
Marcus:	I can't give you away. You aren't one of my things. Your father would be furious, and he'd definitely blame me for everything. Can't Rory just . . . take you?
Julia:	I really wanted to include you Marcus.

Marcus: Thanks, but I'm pretty sure I'll be gone before commencement anyway.

Julia: You will?

Marcus: I've applied to another school. Classes start right away.

Julia: What school?

Marcus: It's . . . The University of Singapore. It's in Singapore.

Julia: What would you be studying there?

Marcus: Singapore, mostly . . . I think.

Julia: What for?

Marcus: To expand the scope of my knowledge. To get another degree.

Julia: Will you be away for a long time?

Marcus: Two years. Three maybe . . . four . . .

Julia: Four years? What'll I do with myself?

Marcus: You'll have Rory to amuse you.

Julia: That's true, but still . . .

Marcus: What?

Julia: Nothing. I think you should go.

Marcus: I don't have to.

Julia: Yes, you do. Go to Singapore. Seize the day!

Marcus: Yeah?

Julia: That's what I'm doing, isn't it?

Marcus: Guess so. *Pause.* Where are you going to live?

Julia: Rory's been offered a position as assistant club pro at a place in the Adirondacks. We thought we'd go there and I could probably give dance lessons to some of the mountain people.

Marcus: I think you're mostly going to meet New Yorkers on holiday.

Julia: Well even better. You know, it turns out that Rory is a pretty fine dancer. A real natural.

Marcus: Better than me?

Julia: I wasn't going to say so, but yeah. About a zillion times.

Marcus: I'm good at the polonaise. You've told me so.

Julia: And I meant it. But all you have to do is walk.

Marcus: With conviction. Oh look . . .

Rory enters, carrying a putter and golf balls.

Julia: Hello Rory.

Rory: Hello Julia. Hello . . . Marcus.

Marcus: Hello Rory. I understand congratulations are in order.

Rory: I guess they are. Hadn't really thought of that.

Julia: What with it being a sort of secret.

Marcus: Ah yes. Well you must be very excited. I know I am.

Rory: Oh, it just slays me. A moment ago I was walking along and I suddenly thought "Shockers delight! In two weeks I'll be a married man!" I'm afraid I had to stop and stand for a second, just to make sure I'd taken it in right.

Julia: You weren't reconsidering?

Rory: No I was just thinking exactly what I said. In two weeks I'll be a married man.

Marcus: Whew!

Rory: *Points at Marcus with his putter and nods gravely.* You know what I mean.

Marcus: Sure.

Rory: And to think, Marcus, I've got you to thank for this turn of events.

Marcus: Oh please . . . don't.

Julia: Rory, I'm not really doing anything at the moment. Would you like to go for a little stroll by the shore?

Rory: Aw Julia, you know I'd like to, but . . . gotta go putt.

Julia: Of course, I understand. Maybe when you're done.

Rory: Maybe. Though I really do have to putt for quite a while.

Julia: Well of course. Some other time. Utterly.

Rory: Right. Well, bye all.

Julia: Bye Rory.

Marcus: Bye bye.

Rory goes out.

Julia: Don't say anything. Alright? Just nothing.

Marcus: I didn't—

Julia: Well you hardly have to.

Marcus: But—

Julia: Nothing! *Pause.* Shockers delight? What the hell does that mean? *They laugh. Rory re-enters.* Oh. Rory.

Rory: Julia, I . . . Excuse me . . . I still want to marry you. I mean, I think I have to say so. So it's clear . . . Even though I've got to go putt . . . You know?

Julia: *Gets up on her knees abruptly.* Of course Rory. I never thought . . . It's sweet of you to say that.

Rory: Well good. *He shifts his weight from side to side, then leans over and kisses her. He stands up and steps back.* Bye again.

Julia: Bye Rory.

Marcus: Bye bye.

Rory goes out. Julia collapses on the ground.

Marcus: Alright, I'm willing to accept a tiny bit of credit for his discovery.

Julia: Hee hee hee.

Marcus: So Julia . . . I could use a little break. Shall we go for a little stroll by the shore?

Julia: Oh ick. Why would anyone want to go down there?

Marcus: Just as I thought, you brazen and lascivious she-thing!

Julia: Call me what you will, for I've no pride left whatsoever.

Marcus gets up, then takes Julia's arm and pulls her to her feet.

Marcus: You're coming for a stroll and you're going to like it. We're going to admire the bulrushes.

Julia: Bulrushes? Now you never mentioned those!

Marcus: There's lot of 'em. And they're pretty tasty!

Julia squeals with delight and they run out smacking their lips.

Scene Six

Rory is making an oral presentation at the head of a classroom. He holds a golf club which he will use periodically to demonstrate his various points.

Rory: The question I've been given is this "Which, in your opinion, is more important to the success of a golf swing . . . the grip or the stance? Keep in mind that there isn't a right answer." Well, my goodness . . .

I think we all know that a good grip is a pretty indispensable thing. You can swing your club with a lot of power, and if you're lucky and blessed you can swing it with grace and beauty too, but if you're not hangin' onto it just so, then that club's just gonna send the little ball any way that it wants to and all your efforts will have been wasted. Personally, I use an interlock grip, and I'd say about ninety-five per cent of golfers do the same. I've seen fellows attempt the full-finger grip with varying degrees of success. Having all eight fingers on the handle might give you more control, but with the interlock grip the left hand always knows what the right hand is doing and vice-versa, so I think the results just have to be a little more consistent.

On the whole, my grip doesn't vary too much whether I'm driving off the tee, pitching from the fairway, or putting on the green. The stance, of course, is another thing. A close stance allows you smoother footwork for your weight shift and pivot. A wide stance helps you maintain balance. Maintaining balance for a long drive is obviously more difficult than for a short pitch. Therefore, as you make your way from the tee to the green, you've just got to reassess and readjust for every single shot. Your stance is just going to have to change.

So the question is asking what is more important. Is it the grip, which is the thing you don't change, or is it the stance, which is the thing you do change. Does the stance support the work you do with the grip, or is the grip merely the final conduit through which the stance becomes the swing?

I could hedge a little here and say that I think this question has been asked to make us realize that both elements are equally important, but I know the question wasn't "Why is this question being asked?" so here goes. I think the thing of value is the thing that stays the same. If everything changed with every single shot you took, then I think you'd never know where you stood in relation to what you were shooting for. And if you don't know where you stand, then your actual stance just doesn't matter a great big heap, does it.

I vote for the grip. Thank you.

Scene Seven

Julia is making an oral presentation in a similar setting. She refers periodically to index cards.

Julia: "Should the woman lead if she is a much stronger dancer than the man?"

I guess it comes down to what these two hope to accomplish by dancing. If they just want to whoop it up and have a good time, it may not matter. If they wish to feel the true satisfaction that comes from mastering an art form, then I'd have to say no. Art cannot be concerned with indulgence of weaknesses. If that seems harsh, let me add that I think there are more creative solutions to this dilemma than the mere transference of responsibility.

In most dances, the man leads. He moves forward as the lady moves backward. He guides her through all turns with the gentle pressure of his right hand. When a step to the side is accompanied by a gentle pressure from the heel of his left hand, it is a signal to open up. Pressure from his fingers is a signal to return to the closed position. Side steps should be directly to the side. Forward and backward steps should be directly forward and backward.

Now, it's quite conceivable that the woman may be able to exert these same small pressures and lead the man through the dance and very few people would be the wiser. This is socially acceptable, but it's not necessarily fair. She is, after all, going backward, and ought not to be expected to guide. Well then, why doesn't she go forward? Why not indeed? I wonder why we're bothering to follow prescribed steps at all, if we're just going to throw tradition out the window. Let's look at the root of this tradition, shall we? Given that in the majority of these cases the man is a little taller than the woman, or at least wider through the shoulders, the image created will always be of a sturdier and heavier object guiding a lighter and more graceful one. If, as sometimes happens, the woman is taller or wider than the man, then it doesn't do either of them any favours to create the impression that she is pushing him around and around.

So, to the option of the woman going forward, I say firmly no. To the option of the woman leading in reverse, I say that this is at best a stopgap measure, the duration of which depends on her willingness to educate her partner. Ultimately the question of leading ought to be irrelevant, as partners come to know one another and learn to accommodate and enhance one another's skills on the dance floor. Truly fine ballroom dancing is, I believe, not so much about executing prescribed steps accurately, but rather it's about communicating impulses which musical rhythms generate within us. If you're in sync with you're partner, your impulses should be the same, and if they're not initially, they may eventually come to be so. I think it's important that we just keep at it and try not to be overly taxed by technical considerations.

Keep the rhythm. Remember the impulses. I think our impulses are what we have to share. Thank you.

Scene Eight
Marcus its alone. He refers to a piece of paper in his hand.

Marcus: Faculty, fellow students, friends . . . I've been asked to speak on behalf of this year's graduates . . . but I'm not going to. I'm going away and I won't be attending commencement. This is a speech I'm never going to give.

He stands.

Many of us will be pleased with ourselves for having gained that thing we call an education. Now we can get on with our lives. We can all face future challenges with confidence because there's nothing we don't know. *Pause.* Oh-oh. That's not true, is it. There are all sorts of things we don't know, because if it were otherwise, we'd all have scored much higher on our final examinations. I'm sure that any one of us who are graduates this year could ask ourselves one simple question and not know the answer to it. "What's the capital of . . . ?" "Who was the founder of . . . ?" or perhaps more philosophically "What do I think about . . . ?" or "Why can't I . . . ?"

And if we put these questions to each other, I think we could collectively bottom out even that little bit sooner. "Why can't you . . . ?" "Don't you have an opinion on . . . ?" "How the hell can you expect to . . . ?" But maybe I'm wrong here. We've been to college, so we know that when someone asks a question we can't answer, we immediately think of a reason why we can't. "Not in the curriculum." "Professor didn't stress those elements." "Didn't study." Some truer than others. All equally acceptable.

No one has taught me how to answer my own questions efficiently and when they come up. I know how to hedge on myself. I learned that early. But I would like to deal with myself in immediate and concrete terms. How, specifically? I'd like to have the option to lie to myself, or more particularly, I'd like to have the option to lie to myself and get away with it.

Toward this end, I have enrolled in a university on the other side of the world. I don't know that they'll attempt to educate me any differently in Singapore than they have here at the University of Continental North America, but I'm confident that the experience will be disorienting in a really immediate and gratifying way. You see, barring the sudden appearance of a solution to the problems I've cited, I think I'm just going to have to find better and better reasons to remain hopelessly confused.

Scene Nine

On a train station platform, Marcus watches as Julia reads over his speech. His luggage is off to one side. When she's done reading, she turns and looks at him.

Julia: Well, it's a good thing no one else will have to sit through this. A moderately bright person might think you were desperately unhappy. Are you?

Marcus: Not my place to say. That'd be indulgent.

Julia: Rory . . . my fiancé . . . says that the future is what we make of it. He says there's a future in everything.

Marcus: Even in History.

Julia: Everything.

Marcus: So? That's what he says. What about it?

Julia: Isn't it great news!

Marcus: I don't think it's true Julia.

Julia: *Sits abruptly on suitcases.* Oh crikey. What now?

Marcus: For you, I don't know. My immediate future is clear at least. I'll get on the train and then transfer to another train and then I'll be home. I'll spend a few days with my Dad and then I'll get on an airplane and fly west and west until I'm as far east as I can go.

Julia: And then?

Marcus: I don't know. Let up.

Julia: Well I wish you weren't going to go.

Marcus: So I could live in the Adirondacks with you and your husband. I could be a waiter or a pool-boy or . . . Hey! I could be a caddy.

Julia: Watch that smart mouth!

Marcus: Go ahead. Punch me again. That's what you feel like, isn't it? You want to kick and punch and scratch.

Julia: Now why is that?

Marcus: Dunno.

Julia: Dunno dunno.

They stare into space.

Marcus: You don't have to wait with me. I brought a book.

Julia: I want to wait.

Marcus: Well good.

Julia: I don't think I have anything more to say. but I might think of something later, and then I'd be burdened with regret.

Marcus: I know what you mean. The prospect of regret makes the future seem like a bit of a pain, doesn't it.

Julia: Just so, Marcus.

Pause.

Marcus: Have you picked a day yet?

Julia: Friday, probably. Maybe Thursday. Wednesday. Tuesday? I think Tuesday might be the best.

Marcus: It's the soonest. Of the four days . . . If that's what you want.

Julia: Yeah.

A train is heard in the distance.

Marcus: Well there's my train, blasting it's horn in the distance.

Julia: Soon it'll be right here.

Marcus: Yup. I guess I'll move my luggage a few inches closer to the platform.

He moves a suitcase a little closer to the platform. She does the same with one other. Abruptly, they embrace.

Marcus: Julia!

Julia: What?

Marcus: Julia . . . Julia . . . *He continues clinging to her, not looking at her face.*

Julia: What? Stop saying my name!

Marcus: Julia, I think I love you more than your fiancé does.

Julia: Well Marcus, I think I may love you more than I love him.

They pull back and stare at each other, wincing. The train sounds, a little nearer now.

Marcus: What do you think we ought to do?

Julia: I don't know. I . . .

They kiss. Explosively. Marcus pulls back.

Marcus: I think you should call off your engagement.

Julia: I can't do that.

Marcus: I'll do it for you.

Julia: No! That would be . . .

Marcus: What?

Julia: Inappropriate.

Marcus: Inappropriate? Your marriage is inappropriate!

Julia: Arrrr . . . Arrrr . . .

Julia claws at the side of her face. Marcus grabs her and they kiss again.

Marcus: Where is he? Where's Rory right now?

Julia: He's on the golf course.

Marcus: I have to tell him! I have to tell him right now!

Another train blast sounds, very near now.

Julia: But Marcus— . . .

Marcus: Tell me not to do it Julia! Tell me and I'll get on the train and we won't ever know what could have been! Tell me!

Julia: *Turns away.* I can't!!

Marcus: I don't want to think this through. I'm going to do it Julia. Watch my stuff. *He runs out.*

Julia: *Turns and stares after him. She cries out in a tiny faraway voice.* No . . . Help . . . Come back . . . Help help . . .

As the train pulls noisily into the station, Julia picks up the suitcases and charges out.

Scene Ten
On the golf course, at the green of the fourteenth hole. The stage is empty for a moment, then Rory's voice is heard in the distance.

Rory: FORE!! *There's a dull, smacking noise and a scream. A golf ball ricochets onto the stage.* Oh my God! No!!

Marcus staggers on, clutching his forehead. He reels about in agony and collapses. Rory runs on, clutching a golf club.

Rory: Marcus? What are you . . . Marcus! Oh God! *He kneels beside Marcus and props him up.* What is it? How bad is it? Marcus! Let me look . . . *He pulls Marcus's hands away from his forehead to reveal a circular red mark above the bridge of his nose. Rory gasps.*

Marcus: Ohh! Oww! Ohhh!

Rory: Is it . . . Can I . . . *He touches the red spot lightly. Marcus screams.* Oh no!

Marcus: *Babbling.* My brain . . . my very brain . . . I see . . . Shockers delight! Shockers delight!

Rory: What?

Marcus: I see every colour that there is. All the colours are dancing! What a merry palette . . . Ahhhhhh . . . *He twists away from Rory and tries to lie in a curled position.*

Rory: Don't lie down Marcus! Marcus, don't!

Julia runs on.

Julia: Marcus! Rory, what's happened?

Rory: I've hit Marcus. I've struck him between the eyes with a golf ball!

Julia: Rory, that's brutal! That's not even civilized! How could you?

Rory: I don't know what you're talking about. It was an accident.

Julia: What?

Rory: I was pitching onto the green from about fifty yards away. I checked the fairway and then I lined up my shot and hit, and suddenly there he was, just running . . . running like he didn't even know where he was going.

Julia: You're supposed to yell something when you hit the ball. Even I know that!

Rory:	Not every time! And I did yell. When I saw him I yelled "Fore!" and you know, if I hadn't, then I don't think he would have turned around and gotten it right in the middle of the forehead!
Marcus:	*Writhing.* All matter is fluid. The elements of the landscape seem to meld. Everything is before me and nothing is where or how it should be. The world is a suitcase poorly packed. It's a cruel start to a man's vacation.
Julia:	What's he talking about?
Rory:	He's hallucinating . . . or he's delirious. He's in shock.
Julia:	What should we do?
Rory:	You stay here. I'll get help.
Julia:	I don't know what to do.
Rory:	Hold onto him. Keep him talking. I don't know. Keep him alive!

Rory runs out. Julia kneels beside Marcus.

Julia:	Marcus? Marcus . . .
Marcus:	I don't even know who's talking to me.
Julia:	It's me Marcus. It's Julia.
Marcus:	Julia Julia Julia Julia . . .
Julia:	*Takes hold of him very carefully.* You've got to keep still now. Keep still and breathe slowly and try to be calm. Can you sit up a little? *She rearranges him carefully so he's still leaning against her. He twitches less, but his face is still contorted in wincing agony.* Is that alright?
Marcus:	Ow. My head! Something's sloshin' around. Where's the lid? Mustn't spill. Don't want to waste my allowance . . .

Julia whimpers. Marcus giggles a little.

Marcus: My tongue's all heavy. The conversation must suffer as a result. You Julia . . .

Julia: Yes?

Marcus: Julia Julia Julia Julia, you should talk to me about something.

Julia: Well I . . . I . . .

Marcus: *Clutches her desperately.* Talk! Talk . . .

Julia: I . . . The . . . The dance which we currently know as the waltz had its origins in the round dances and laendlers of Tyrolean peasantry, but it's widespread social acceptance did not come about until the end of the Biedermeier era.

Marcus: Biedermeier . . . I know that . . . Bieder . . . meier . . .

Julia: *Sobs.* Oh Marcus . . .

Marcus: Biedermeier Biedermeier Biedermeier Biedermeier . . .

Slow Fade

ACT TWO

Scene One

Six years later. Rory is sitting at a mid-size Biedermeier style table, wiping beer steins with a towel. He wears an apron overtop a shirt, vest, and trousers typical of the early nineteenth century. Marcus enters, dressed similarly, but with a jacket and cloth satchel.

Marcus: Ah, good day to you, my fine fellow.

Rory: And good day to you sir.

Marcus: I query, have I found myself to the famous Inn of the Golden Antlers?

Rory: You have sir, and I am the merry innkeeper. Will you sit and raise a tankard, oh stranger?

Marcus: Certainly I will, and I'll hope also to break a loaf of pumpernickel with you my good man.

Rory: I've no pumpernickel about, I'm sorry to say.

Marcus: Well I've some here in my satchel. Ha-ha!

Rory: Ha-ha! Sit down at my table then, oh guest of the Golden Antlers!

Marcus sits and takes out a loaf of bread which he places on the table. Rory sets down two beer steins and sits.

Marcus: I do. I sit and I admire the table, for it seems most lucid and unpretentious in design.

Rory: I thank you for taking note of its quality, for it is a most precious acquisition. It cost me dearly and it's modern to boot.

Marcus: Indeed it is. Your table seems to typify the very tenor of our era.

Rory: What era is this, good stranger? I am a mere innkeeper of

the Rhineland and rely upon my visitors for enlighten-
ment as to the developments in all the German Provinces
and in Austria too.

Marcus: My good man, this is the era which will be called the time
of Biedermeier and it's your table which stands at the centre of the universe just now.

Rory: My table? But this is beyond my comprehension. What of
the worship of nature which has been such a caution of
late?

Marcus: Innkeeper see! See in this simple table an extension of
this worship. We who are romantic by nature would celebrate the tree, but those whose romanticism is informed
by pragmatism, and I am of that number . . . We know
that the tree must fall. And yet . . . And so . . . We celebrate
the board.

Rory: The board, which though planar, is no less a part of the
tree than bark or branches. I see!

Marcus: The surface is so smooth, the corners simple and
unadorned by sculptural elements.

Rory: In truth guest, some have thought my table plain.

Marcus: Plain? Philistines I cry, and now I drain this tankard, lest
I lose my even temper and fulminate unduly against this
outrageous charge.

*He takes several big gulps from his stein. Rory does the same. Marcus sets
his stein down and kneels before the table.*

Marcus: See, friend. Here are traces of exquisite ornament which
are the more telling for their discretion. Look here . . . the
battens . . .

Rory: Yes, what of the battens?

Marcus: They have no tectonic function.\

Rory: So they're just . . .

Marcus: There. They're simply there.

Rory: *Embraces the table.* Oh thing of value!

Marcus: But enough of this. Enough of the furniture! Tell me, where in these parts may I find the dwelling of Hostess Braunschweig?

Rory: What? Are you acquainted with that lady?

Marcus: I cast my eyes down as I say "Yes." And know that this act must illuminate the very truth of our acquaintance.

Rory: But Hostess Braunschweig has fled these parts. She has taken herself up and away. Her cottage stands empty, her garden gone to rack and ruin.

Marcus: Oh schmerz!

Rory: How we all do miss her merry temperament and lively parties.

Marcus: I'll go to her house and see her overgrown garden.

Rory: You'll scarcely find it, for it is nearly one with the surrounding forest.

Marcus: Good innkeeper, I'll know. Not all blossoms are alike to me. I'll know the branch from which she plucked, and then I'll pluck there too. Pluck-pluck.

Rory: I wish you well guest, and must inquire as to your name.

Marcus: I am Otto von Pfadschlepper.

Rory: The rural economist?

Marcus: Once, yes . . . but no more.

He collapses at the table. Rory approaches and looks on quizzically.

Rory: Herr von Pfadschlepper . . . Otto . . . Will you have some pumpernickel?

Marcus sits up slowly.

Marcus: I'm very tired now Rory.

Rory: Sure you are Marcus. We'll just stop. You go have a little sleep and I'll put the things away.

Marcus: *Stands.* The things . . . There's bread and cups. That's not many things so it's okay. I'll just go and have a little sleep. Can you untie my neck for me Rory?

Rory: Sure. *He undoes the ties attached to Marcus's shirt collar.*

Marcus: It's too easy for me to tie them and keep tying them by accident and then I can't breathe.

Rory: Well I don't mind undoing them. There ya go. All done.

Marcus: Thank you very much Rory.

Rory: You're welcome.

Marcus: Good night.

Rory: See ya later.

Marcus: Hey! It's not night at all. This is afternoon. S*peaks as he goes.* So many millions of times for things to happen in. The times all go around like crazy.

Rory watches Marcus leave, then clears the table and exits.

Scene Two
The dance classroom, as seen in Act One. Julia enters. She stands and looks around, then crosses slowly and peruses the charts and looks at the stack of records. She selects one and puts it on. It's the merengue, and as it plays, she walks slowly around the room. The music is quite loud and she doesn't notice when Rory enters.

Rory: I beg your pardon. What's—

Julia:	*Turns.* What?
Rory:	Julia?
Julia:	Oh my. Rory.

They stare at one another for a moment. She goes to the record player and lifts the needle, cutting off the music. She turns and smiles faintly.

Rory:	Well well. Shockers delight.
Julia:	You said it.
Rory:	What are you doing here?
Julia:	Here? I'm reminiscing.
Rory:	I mean here. You've come back to UCNA. What for? Where have you been?
Julia:	Singapore.
Rory:	For six years?
Julia:	There's lots to do there. I got another degree. I studied Economic Theory and Practice in the Malay Peninsula. I did that for four years and then I got a job in a dance hall. I worked at that for two years and now I've come back. My mother told me that Marcus was still living here and that he's living with you. Is that right?
Rory:	Yes it is. Marcus is doing very well, though he can't quite . . . take care of himself. He's very healthy. He's . . . He's just not right. He isn't ever going to be right. That's something you'd better know.
Julia:	Okay.
Rory:	After the accident . . . Well, after he got out of the hospital and started in rehabilitation—
Julia:	Which was when?

Rory: Three months I think. You'd been gone a fair while. Well it got to be obvious things had changed and his father sued me for a whole lot of money.

Julia: Oh no . . .

Rory: And he won and I think he should have won because I damaged his son's brain and none of us could look at it any other way. So my parents paid the money out of my trust fund. They weren't ruined by it, but we were out of pocket for a little while. I made it clear though, that I didn't just want to give money to Marcus. I wanted to help him in any way that I could, and I wanted to see him and talk to him and not forget him, either as he was or as he is.

Julia turns away.

Rory: I'm sorry Julia. I didn't mean anything by that. Anyway . . . Two years ago Mr. Whitelaw died but before he did, he asked me if I would be Marcus's legal guardian. Of course I accepted, and I brought him back here.

Julia: But that must make it hard for you to golf. You wouldn't be able to tour on the pro circuit or—

Rory: Julia, I haven't hit a golf ball since that day. How could I? I know what I'd be thinking every time I went to swing. I'd want to look and see if there was someone there. Someone in danger . . . from me. And you can't be doing that. You have to keep your eye on the ball.

Julia: So you've given it up? But it was what you studied. It was what you did. It was who you were.

Rory: It was just golf. I do something else now. After six years it's no big deal.

Julia: What do you do?

Rory: I teach ballroom dancing. I went through the program here and then I stayed on. This is my classroom.

Julia:	My God, if you've trained you must be pretty stunning now.
Rory:	I don't know that I had to improve much. Learning the names of all the dances . . . That was torture.
Julia:	I'm really out of practice. I was just listening to the merengue and thinking I don't even know how it starts anymore.
Rory:	But you said you spent two years in a dance hall.
Julia:	It wasn't the sort of place where dancing was a priority. The gentlemen would buy tickets and then they'd just cling to you and you'd sort of shuffle back and forth till a bell sounded and they'd have to give you another ticket and you'd just keep at it till they ran out. Of course, there were other things you could do for tips, but I never bothered. It wasn't as though it'd have been big money.
Rory:	Why would you do that at all? If you had a degree in Economic Theory there must have been some good jobs you'd have been qualified for.
Julia:	Sure, but I didn't want them. It was an interesting field, but it's not like I was ever really interested, you know? And I wasn't really miserable at the dance hall. I got to wear a lot of great outfits. Little satin cocktail dresses, sort of exotic and slutty at the same t—
Rory:	*Abruptly and intensely.* Julia, why did you go? Why have you come back?
Julia:	I came back because I wanted to say I was sorry.
Rory:	To who? To me?
Julia:	To you, to Marcus . . . To anyone I can get hold of.
Rory:	I don't understand. You're sorry that you went away?
Julia:	Definitely not. I had to go away. There was no choice for

me. Maybe I'm sorry about that. Maybe I'm just sorry that things got so bad all of a sudden.

Rory: So . . . You're saying you don't even know what you're—

Julia: Look, Rory, does it really matter? I felt bad. I still do. I wish I didn't. I'm sorry!

Rory: You felt bad? Listen, it's not so much that I beaned Marcus in the face and wrecked his life forever . . . That's not what gets me. I remember thinking as I started out that afternoon that he was going to be leaving in a few hours, and I was so happy about that because it meant I'd finally have you all to myself. I hardly knew Marcus, but I was pretty sure I didn't like him. He made me nervous because being around him reminded me that I hardly knew you, and when I saw the two of you together I always felt like you couldn't wait for me to leave so you could laugh about some private thing. So I was glad he was going. I was just so glad, and then there he was on the golf course, obviously looking for me, and I can only think he'd come to say goodbye.

I think I misjudged him completely and so I guess I misjudged you too, and when you left a few days later, I didn't blame you at all. Now, I don't mean to say "Top that," or anything, but you've come halfway across the world to say you're sorry for something, only you can't quite say what it is and I don't get it!

Julia: Oh, Rory . . .

She turns and starts to walk away from him, nearly colliding with Marcus, who is entering. Julia steps back with a little cry.

Marcus: Oh.

Julia: Hello . . . there . . .

Marcus: *Nods.* Hi.

Julia and Marcus stare at each other.

Marcus: You're staring.

Julia: *Looks away.* I'm sorry.

Marcus: You're crying.

Julia: No . . . I'm not . . .

Marcus: You are. You're a dancing lady.

Julia: No. Not really.

Rory: Marcus, this is Julia. She's just been visiting me.

Marcus: Julia's visiting?

Rory: Yes.

Marcus: Julia . . .

Julia: Yes?

Marcus: Stop crying. Rory, I want eggs for supper.

Rory: We had eggs for breakfast.

Marcus: But they were good and there's still some in the refriger-ator. That's what I want today.

Rory: I think we should have something else.

Marcus: But we don't have anything else. It's smart to have eggs.

Rory: We can buy some chicken. How about that?

Marcus: I'll have to think about it. *Gravely.* It's quite a different thing to eat.

Rory: Well how about I give you some money and you go see Hilda at the butcher's and buy a chicken—

Marcus: But I don't—

Rory: And when I get home, we can put the chicken on the table and look at it and we'll just think about whether we want to eat it.

Marcus: We might not want to.

Rory: Then we'll have eggs. How's that?

Marcus: It's a good idea Rory. I'll buy the chicken.

Rory: *Hands him bills.* Here's some money then.

Marcus: This is to pay for the chicken, Julia. Hilda sells chickens at the butcher's.

Julia: Yes, I remember Hilda.

Marcus: I remember Hilda too. I always do, but lots of other people I forget over and over again. I can't help it Julia.

Julia: Well, you've remembered my name.

Marcus: Yeah, that's good. I have to go. I'd better go quick in case Hilda closes the butcher's.

Rory: It's early Marcus. You've still got lots of time.

Marcus: It's important not to waste time, even when you've got a lot of it. It's important not to waste time if you sometimes forget what you're doing. Goodbye Rory. Goodbye Julia.

Rory: Bye Marcus.

Julia: Bye bye.

Marcus: Julia, you should ask Rory if you can be a dancing lady. He's a very good dancer. He can teach you to dance so that anyone would want to be your partner. Go on . . . *He nods at her pointedly and then goes out, clutching the money in his fist.*

There's a substantial pause before Julia murmurs quietly.

Julia: That was Marcus Whitelaw. My Marcus . . . Is he always like that?

Rory: Pretty much. He's not always that relaxed in front of strangers . . . Or people he doesn't remem—

Julia chokes and turns away.

Rory: It's hard. I know it is.

Julia: He's like an earnest little boy.

Rory: Yeah.

Julia: He was never earnest before. Never in his life. When we were kids he was pushy and mean.

Rory: Julia, does the Biedermeier Era mean anything to you?

Julia: What?

Rory: Biedermeier. Do you know anything about it?

Julia: A bit. Probably more than you'd rightly expect me to.

Rory: Not more than me, I'll bet. I've had to do a lot of readin' up.

Julia: I don't see—

Rory: Biedermeier makes Marcus different. It can focus his thoughts and make him strong and well. For limited amounts of time.

Julia: Biedermeier. Furniture?

Rory: The furniture, the whole kit 'n' kaboodle.

Julia: I'm lost.

Rory: I'd like you to come to our house Julia.

Julia: Sure . . .

Rory: Not for another day or two. We'll need time to get you an outfit.

Julia: Yeah?

Rory: And I'll explain.

Julia: Great.

He clasps her hand.

Rory: I'm glad to see you Julia. I'm really glad.

Julia: Well . . . I'm glad to be here.

Rory: And what a party there'll be at the Inn of the Golden Antlers!

Julia raises an eyebrow.

Scene Three
At Marcus and Rory's home, two days later. Marcus sits at the table in his Biedermeier costume.

Marcus: Innkeeper! Innkeeper I say! Bring me a tankard of your best!

Rory: *Offstage.* Forthwith, my friend. And speedily!

Marcus: And I entreat you, draw a tankard for yourself. We'll sit and quaff the nut-brown ale together.

Rory: Ha-ha-ha!

He enters wearing his apron as before and carrying beer steins.

Marcus: Ha-ha!

They clunk their steins together.

Marcus: I thank you my good man and inquire, what is your Christian name?

Rory: I'm called Fritz, sir.

Marcus: Fritz? A good name for a good man. To your very good health Fritz!

Rory: Ha-ha!

They clunk glasses a second time.

Marcus: It seems a quiet night here at The Inn of the Golden Antlers.

Rory: Indeed, there are few citizens in need of my hospitality this evening. And yet . . . And yet, I feel some sort of excitement stirring . . . A premonition of some unexpected revelation.

Marcus: A premonition of what is unexpected? Your speech confounds, good Fritz. And further, I give no credit to premonitions of any sort, for I am a rural economist. I view nature with respect, but also with appreciation of its commercial import. Today sheep, tomorrow mutton . . . You know the sort of thing.

Rory: Indeed, you display the new pragmatism which moulds our era.

Marcus: But what a struggle it is Fritz. I am not so sensible by inclination as I might like to be. Why here in my heart—

Julia clears her throat offstage.

Marcus: But what was that?

Rory: A knock, Herr von Pfadschlepper. I believe it was a knock.

There is a faint "Oh" offstage, followed by a knock.

Marcus: It seems there's to be another guest here at the inn. How . . . rare.

Rory: I'll look to the door. *He goes to the doorway, then steps back.* But what do I see? Unexpected revelation indeed. Come in, my good dame!

Julia enters in a full Biedermeier gown.

Marcus: Dame? What dame is it?

Rory: Look and see. surely you must recognize the sorely missed and pined for—

Marcus: Can it be? You are then—

Rory: It is Hostess Braunschweig, returned from abroad.

Julia: Hello.

Marcus: My eyes deceive me. It cannot be. You are an apparition, Madame.

Julia: No I'm not.

Marcus: Yes. Yes, you are.

Julia: No I'm not. I'm Hostess Braunschweig.

Rory: It's true Otto. See . . . *Pokes Julia.* A tiny poke verifies that she's no apparition.

Marcus advances hesitantly and gives Julia a little poke.

Marcus: Well then, I marvel. I marvel at your return. *Kneels before her.* I kiss your hand Hostess and welcome you most heartily to The Inn of the Golden Antlers. but please, I beg to know of your whereabouts these past—

Rory: Please, Herr von Pfadschlepper, the lady has been travelling and is no doubt in need of some refreshment. Ale, Hostess?

Marcus: Ale's not suitable Fritz. The lady must have sack.

Julia: Sack?

Rory: Certainly! Sack it shall be.

He hands Julia a glass. She looks at him quizzically. He shrugs.

Marcus: We hoist our tankards to the return of Hostess Braunschweig. Prosit!

All: Prosit!

They drink.

Marcus: Is it to your liking Madame?

Julia: It's strong . . . But not too strong. It's just right . . . Isn't it?

Rory: I've had an inspiration. Perhaps to make the festive mood complete, the good hostess will now lead us in one of the lively dances for which her parties were once so widely celebrated.

Julia: But I'm not finished my sack.

Marcus: Yes yes. A dance will be good fun. But there's no orchestra here at the inn.

Rory: I think earlier I spied an itinerant group of musicians in the courtyard. Perhaps they can be induced to play. *Calls off.* What ho fellows! Have you some music for us? *Turns back.* They'll play for some small coin.

Julia: Ask if they'd like some sack.

Marcus: *Tosses Rory a coin.* Here's a ducat.

Rory: Aha! *He runs off.*

Marcus: Hostess Braunschweig, now that we're alone, I beg of you—

The sound of a record needle dropping heavily is heard and a merry Biedermeier dance is heard.

Julia: Come Otto, we'll dance now and talk a little later.

Marcus: Of course. I readily acquiesce.

Rory returns and Julia leads the men in a twirling thigh-slapping dance of the Biedermeier period. All applaud merrily at the conclusion and another piece begins to play.

Marcus: Please, friend Fritz, go now and bid the band to play more quietly. I can no longer wait for a private interview with this lady. *Gives coins to Rory.* Another ducat for the band and one for your own trouble.

Rory: You are most generous sir. Hostess, are you agreeable to my temporary absence?

Julia: Why yes Innkeeper. I am beholden to you for your solicitude, but I can have no trepidation where Herr von Pfadschlepper is concerned.

Rory: I will withdraw then.

He bows and backs out of the room. After a moment, the music becomes quieter, but continues to play.

Marcus: More sack, Hostess?

Julia: No thank you. I feel I must retain my wits just now. And please, Otto, you must feel free to address me by my given name.

Marcus: With pleasure Hostess, but I don't know what that is.

Julia: Oh . . . It's . . . Elfi . . .

Marcus: Elfi. That's sweet and magical. The diminutive of . . .

Julia: Elfinborg.

Marcus: Please Elfi, come sit with me at the table. Have you taken note of the table? See how smooth it is, and true to nature.

Julia:	So free of spurious adornment. I would be this table if I could.
Marcus:	That's not so fantastical a desire as one might presume, for the future of our era is so close to human scale. But Elfi . . . I would . . . I must . . .
Julia:	What is it Otto? Speak freely.
Marcus:	My thoughts are disordered and my words can't hope to do them justice. Indeed my lips tremble and cannot do justice to the words. Elfi . . . Do you remember that afternoon when we stood by the coach house?
Julia:	Why . . . Yes Otto. of course I remember it.
Marcus:	Then let my lips importune without further recourse to words. Elfi . . . *He seizes her and kisses her on the mouth. She pulls back briefly, but he pulls her to him and kisses her again. She gives in completely and is melting into his arms, when she suddenly pulls back and crosses away from him.*
Julia:	No! I can't!
Marcus:	Alas! Hostess . . . Elfi . . . Why do you reject me when by doing so you must clearly contravene the desires of your own heart?
Julia:	I fear . . . I think my heart is too small.
Marcus:	I think it must be exquisite.
Julia:	Perhaps that's so, but it's not strong enough to contain the quantity of desires which move me. My heart is over-filled Otto, and so it cannot love well.
Marcus:	I think you're telling me . . . that you do still love another.

Rory stands in the doorway unobserved.

Julia:	I do. That's the painful truth, just as I told it to you that day at the coach house.

Marcus: You'll forgive me if I recall your kiss more clearly. I hold that it spoke with greater force and clarity than you could contrive with your wits.

Julia: That may be so, but I am betrothed. I am betrothed to another.

Marcus: To whom? Tell me his name.

Julia: I cannot.

Marcus: Does he love you more than I do?

Julia: How can I ever really know?

Marcus: Do you love him more than you love me?

Julia: I don't know. These questions are unfair.

Marcus: Why do you stay betrothed to him if you don't know any of these things?

Julia: Because I feel like it. Damn it Marcus, I wish I could make it all logical for you, but I just can't!

Marcus stares at Julia, then sits down abruptly. He looks very confused.

Julia: Otto?

Marcus shakes his head and turns away. Rory steps into the room. Julia looks from one to the other, then gestures for Rory to leave. He looks questioningly at her, but she nods assertively and he goes. Julia approaches Marcus and stands behind him. She puts her arms around him gently and rests her chin on the top of his head.

Marcus: *Hazily.* Who's that? What are you doing?

Julia: Otto, do you remember the day we stopped outside of Koblenz and looked down into the valley where the Mosel meets the Rhine? Do you remember that?

Marcus: I don't know.

Julia: You spoke of nature.

Marcus: I think . . . I think I always do.

Julia: You said we had much to learn from nature, and not so much from its beauty as from its sense. You said that the Mosel was a very fine river, but it had enough wisdom not to try to make headway from something so formidable as the Rhine. And so it gave itself up and made the Rhine into something greater.

Marcus: I do remember this. And you said it was still a pity because there are other regions where the Rhine is so small and piddling that the Mosel might overwhelm it easily.
Julia: But that's not what happens. They meet at Koblenz and so we see what we see.

Marcus: *Quietly.* Elfi, why are you marrying this other man instead of me?

Julia: Because he asked me first.

Marcus: And that's the only reason?

Julia: It's the one I understand best.

Marcus considers for a moment, then takes out a small vial.

Marcus: Elfi, I'd like to present you with this small vial.

Julia: What is it Otto? Some sort of perfume?

Marcus: No, these are the tears I shed for you in your absence. You may keep them as a reminder of one who loved you with more folly than wisdom.

Julia: I will keep these tears and look at them as a tribute and a caution to myself. And I will love you too Otto, no less than I have ever done.

Marcus: Secretly . . .

Julia:	Privately, but not clandestinely.
Marcus:	Please, when may I learn the identity of the fortunate man who commands your heart?
Julia:	Soon Otto. Perhaps before the morning steals upon the night.
Marcus:	And will you never more stray from The Inn of the Golden Antlers?
Julia:	You come too close to asking too many questions.
Marcus:	I'll gaze upon you one last time Hostess, and then you must close my eyes.
Julia:	Of course.

He looks at her, smiling a little. She crosses and touches his eyelids gently and he shuts them. She stands back a little and looks at him.

Julia:	Otto . . .

He shakes his head.

Julia:	Marcus?
Marcus:	I'm really sleepy now. That's always how it gets.
Julia:	Are you going to bed now? Do you need help?
Marcus:	No. *He opens his eyes and gets up slowly.* But can you untie my ties?
Julia:	Of course I can.
Marcus:	For me it's always fuss fuss fuss and then I can't breathe.
Julia:	*Pulls out the knot.* There you go.
Marcus:	Thank you . . . Julia.
Julia:	You're welcome Marcus.

Marcus: Rory never minds to put the things away.

Julia: I'm sure it's fine. You just go to bed.

Marcus: Good night . . . Julia.

Julia: Good night Marcus.

She bends forward and kisses the tip of his nose. He giggles and wipes it with his hand. He turns to go and sees the vial on the table. He picks it up and holds it out to her.

Marcus: All that's in here is water. You can pour it down the drain.

She takes it from him and he goes out. She looks at the vial, then presses it to her lips and lowers it and holds it over her heart.

Scene Four
On the fourteenth green of the golf course, later that night. Rory wanders on. He looks at the flag, circling around it slowly. He stops and squats and feels the short grass, and then lies down on his back. He spreads his arms and legs wide, then moves them around slowly. Julia approaches, wearing an overcoat. She stands and watches him awhile before speaking quietly.

Julia: Fore.

Rory: *Sits up.* Wha . . . Oh. Hello Julia.

Julia: Good evening.

Rory: How did you know I was here?

Julia: Didn't. I just thought of a few likely places. This one seemed like it'd be the most appealing at this time of night. I've always loved golf courses in the middle of the night.

Rory: I know what you mean. They're like big deserted parks that no one thinks to go to.

Julia: This used to be one of our favourite places to drink. Marcus and I . . . *Takes out a flask.* Care to join me? It's whisky.

Rory: You bet. Got any crackers?

Julia: No, do you believe it? You get older, you start to let things go. There's no excuse though. Crackers are pretty readily available.

She takes a swig and hands him the flask. He drinks.

Rory: Everything's alright at The Inn of the Golden Antlers?

Julia: I think it is. Hostess Braunschweig has successfully declined the suit of Otto von Pfadschlepper.

Rory: Ah. That's probably for the best.

Julia: Do you want to know what she told him.

Rory: I think . . . whatever it was should remain between the two of them.

Julia: Indeed. You're right.

She has another swig of whisky.

Rory: He's probably very disappointed.

Julia: He will be, but I foresee a greater flowering of his genius now that he can devote himself unequivocally to the worship of furniture and by extension, the natural world. Were you worshipping the natural world just now? Is that why you're lying here?

Rory: I don't think there's anything very natural about a putting green. I've always wondered what it would be like to lie on one. We were always taught to respect the green. Don't wear your cleats on it.Don't walk on it any more than you absolutely have to. But it always seemed so soft and sort of . . . downy and inviting. *He lies back down.*

Julia:	And how is it?
Rory:	I'm really liking it. *Pats the ground beside him.* Why don't you try?
Julia:	Well . . . I suppose . . . *She sits down and then lies rather carefully.* If I seem to be doing this rather carefully, it's because I haven't got anything on under this coat.
Rory:	Ha . . . What?
Julia:	When I put my gown on I guess I left my clothes in Marcus's room. He went in to sleep and I didn't want to wake him. It's a nice night, no big deal.
Rory:	That's my coat.
Julia:	Well you can't have it back. Not just yet.
Rory:	Sure, whenever.
Julia:	It's a bit wet here on the green, isn't it.
Rory:	They water it several times a day.
Julia:	It feels like dew.
Rory:	Some trick huh?

Pause.

Julia:	Rory, have you . . . It might not be any of my business, but have their been any . . . other girls since I left?
Rory:	Well . . . not really . . . really . . .
Julia:	None of your dancing ladies. Not one or two or—
Rory:	Three or four? Well, maybe, just . . . but not . . .
Julia:	What?

Rory: I never liked necking with them. It always left me feeling sad.

Julia: Sad? Why?

Rory shrugs.

Rory: And what about you?

Julia: Not too many dates. Dance hall girls kinda lose the impetus. There were two or three, but yeah . . . It made me sad. I didn't blame the necking so much, maybe because I was in a foreign country and I was working as white slave trash. I didn't mind being a little sad. It seemed sort of sweet.

Rory: Well not to me. I thought it was debilitating and stupid. After a while I just wouldn't put myself through it. I've had other things to think about. Taking care of Marcus, teaching—

Julia: You're a little smarter than I am Rory.

Rory: Oh, doubt it.

Julia: You are. Just a little. Don't think I'm not irritated by that.

Rory: Okay. *He rolls over onto his stomach.*

Julia: What are you doing?

Rory: My back's all wet. Might as well do the whole outfit.

Julia: Makes sense. *She rolls over. They lie on their stomachs for a moment.* This is very nice. Bit hard to breathe though.

Rory: *Muffled.* I'd have to agree.

He rolls over toward her. She does the same. They roll again. She rolls on top of him and they roll again so that he's on top of her.

Rory: Do you really have nothing at all on under this coat?

Julia:	Oh, wouldn't ya like to know.
Rory:	Yeah.
Julia:	Well the point is . . . I'm not dressed. Use your imagination.
Rory:	Mmmm . . .
Julia:	No don't.
Rory:	But—
Julia:	But nothing!

She pulls his head down and they kiss. They roll over, still kissing, so she ends up on top. She pulls away.

Julia:	That make ya sad?
Rory:	Nope.

They kiss again. Julia stops.

Julia:	Now . . . We're going to do this again, aren't we? Tomorrow, I mean . . . and maybe . . . sometime next week?
Rory:	I think . . . it's not unlikely.
Julia:	Then I'm going to suggest we not linger here on the cold wet grass.
Rory:	*Gets up.* I think that's a fairly smart suggestion.
Julia:	It's a relief to know we're not insatiable.

They look at each other then abruptly kiss with more heat than before. They break away slowly.

Julia:	Someone had better change the topic fairly quickly.
Rory:	Gosh, what do you think par is here at the fourteenth hole?

Julia: Well . . . This is the back nine, right?

Rory: Right.

Julia: Well then . . . How should I know what par is? I know nothing of golf.

Rory: It's four.

Julia: That so? Hm. *Looks around.* You know, I think if I were a golfer, I'd prefer to play at night.

Rory: I think that'd be hard. You'd tee off and then probably . . . just wander. You'd never know if you were anywhere near the green.

Julia: I'd have a lot of faith in myself.

Rory: You know Julia, I think you should take up golf.

Julia: Why? I'd be nervous about hitting people after what you told me.

Rory: I'd spot for you. I'd caddy. Really, I've got a whole set of clubs just gathering dust.

Julia: Don't think so.

Rory: They're really expensive.

Julia: Well I suppose I might need some sort of activity for the rest of my life. A career . . . I might need one of those.

Rory: I remember when marriage was your main goal.

Julia: Well it was, but then I heard the most outrageous thing.

They start to exit.

Rory: What's that?

Julia: Apparently for some women it's just not enough.

Rory: Is that a fact? Interesting . . .

They wander off, still chatting in this vein.

Scene Five
Rory is speaking at a podium.

Rory: Recently, one of my students asked me the following question. "In ballroom dancing, which is more important . . . the footwork, or the carriage of the upper body?" I asked her why one had to be more important than the other. "Well I want to know which to work on more." I'm not sure that this is the soundest approach to getting an education and I told her so. I am willing to speculate though, on why one is not more important than the other.

The footwork that you do in any given dance is what makes it unique. The mambo steps are different from the samba steps and the waltz is different from the polka. It's the most technical and scientific aspect of ballroom dancing, because it involves counting. You count the rhythm of the music and select the steps accordingly. You don't do the lindy if they're playing the cha-cha. You can't, because it doesn't fit.

So, you've analysed the music and selected the appropriate steps. You get into position with your partner and you execute these steps. Technically, you're dancing. But the music is telling you much more than simply what you ought to do with your feet. If that was the whole point, we could just beat blocks of wood together and not have to hire a band. The music should be communicating a sense of emotion, and you should too. That is what the rest of your body is for.

Now, maintaining the correct sequence of steps is not a variable. You have to do it, even though it's liable to limit what you're able to accomplish above the waist. You'll be able to lean a little to emphasize a phrase, or you might add a bit of a flourish to a turn or to an open and close. On the whole though, you'll find the steps come more easily if you're able to maintain a poised upper body. Please note, this should not be seen as a compromise. Fancy footwork combines with a poised carriage and the result is graciousness. Make no mistake, to be dancing is to be under pressure, so grace is a pretty good thing to have. You can show grace in how you align yourself with your partner, and in how you lead and how you follow. I think, ultimately, the steps are what make the dance, but it's the poise which makes the dancer.

I explained all of this to my student and she said it sounded to her like I'd actually made a choice. I said we'd better change the subject or the point would be lost. She then brought up the question of The Beatles and other groups of that ilk. She asked how you were supposed to dance to their music while thinking about your upper body alignment. I guess it's worth remembering that there are occasional situations in the ballroom where it's just best to throw poise out the window for a bit. But I'm hoping these dances aren't going to become prevalent.

Scene Six
Julia stands at the podium. She is stylishly attired, as a golfer.

Julia: I'm supposed to explain the appeal of golf in our time. I've only been enrolled in the golf program here for a month, so I guess there's a chance that what I have to say might be naive or at least unsophisticated. I think that's fine, because we're talking about an outdoor sport.

I'm a pretty restless woman. But when I play golf, I find it's just not as easy to be restless. You walk and you stand, you walk and you stand, and every so often you get to hit something really hard. I thought maybe this last element was the most appealing to me, so I spent an afternoon at the driving range, only to find it a curiously unsatisfying experience. Ball after ball would fly out into the field and lie there with all the others. I kept hitting more and more buckets of them, thinking it might all add up to something, but it never did.

So I guess what I know is that I like the walking and I like the standing, and I really like the hitting . . . but the ball has to go into the hole. The ball goes into the hole and then you know without question that it's time to move on to to the next tee. And when you finally reach the eighteenth green and sink your last putt, you know you've done all you can. Whether or not you've made par, or scored higher or lower than your opponents, you've still done what you came to do. You've made the ball go into the hole. And that's terrific.

Scene Seven

Marcus sits in the rowboat in the middle of the lake. He's wearing his Biedermeier costume and holding a diary and a pen.

Marcus: Today, I am beginning my diary. This book has been given to me by my friend Hostess Braunschweig, who has suggested that my thoughts and observations are somewhat singular and worthy of preservation. I don't know that I concur, but I am devoted to Elfi and I will make this effort in order to please her, and to see if she's correct.

I am writing now in a little rowboat floating on the lake that's down the road from The Inn of the Golden Antlers, where I live. I must note that Elfi has now revealed to me the identity of her betrothed, and it is none other than Fritz, the keeper of the inn. I was most startled by this, but relieved as well, for Fritz is the very best of men. This revelation has strengthened my resolve to cast aside the passion which once raged within me, for to declare my love for Elfi would bring grief to Fritz, who has been the kindest and most hospitable of friends.

Fritz and Elfi have just recently procured a fine new piece of furniture and they have presented it to me as a gift. It's a bureau-cabinet, designed in the very best style of the day. It's so rectangular and so solid, and it's made of long sheets of beautiful light wood, with the only ornament being a small Grecian lyre inlaid at each corner of the front. I love my new bureau-cabinet and every morning when I awake it's the first thing I see, and it immediately gives me such a strong sense of the world in which I live and the time in which I live there. I should say too that it is a great convenience for storing my things, and the functional nature of the piece may yet turn out to be the most profoundly praiseworthy of its aspects.

I am most content at this moment, in my boat on the little lake. It's quite peaceful here, and that ought to be odd. The boat rocks after all, and changes direction of its own accord, and the flimsy construction of the vessel really does seem to leave it ill-equipped to keep me from sinking into the water below. Still, it manages, and through this small artifice I am allowed to be at one with nature. I see this as a paradox of the modern world, and floating too seems to me to be most paradoxical. Whether an object floats on the water or on the breezes, its situation is quite precarious, yet peaceful at the same time.

Rory and Julia appear on the shore in Biedermeier costume. They smile and wave at Marcus, then set about laying out a picnic.

Marcus: Right now I see Fritz and Elfi waving to me from the shore. Soon I'll row in and we'll have a splendid picnic with fresh bread and cold meats and very fine cheese. But I am loathe to leave my spot here on the lake. And I don't think my friends will be too put out by having to spend a few more moments alone together. And so I put my diary down. I put aside all my reflections. I close my eyes and scarcely breathe. I am at peace, and so I float.

He sits back in the boat with his eyes closed. On the shore, Julia reclines in Rory's arms as they sit on the picnic blanket.

Slow Fade

*Davina Stewart as Virginia Tilford, Jeff Haslam as Jack Vail,
and Leona Brausen as Nancy Kimble in the Teatro La Quindicina
production of* Pith!, *Edmonton, Alberta, 1999.*

Photo: Peter Edwards

Pith!

Production History

Pith! was first produced by Teatro La Quindicina at the Edmonton Fringe Festival in August, 1997.
The production was revived at High Performance Rodeo in Calgary and at the Varscona Theatre in Edmonton in January, 1999. A revival, featuring the original cast will open at the Varscona Theatre in May, 2004.

C A S T

Jack Vail	*Jeff Haslam*
Mrs. Virginia Tilford	*Davina Stewart*
Miss Nancy Kimble	*Leona Brausen*

Director	*Stewart Lemoine*
Coistume Designer	*Leona Brausen*

Production Notes

C H A R A C T E R S

Jack Vail: an itinerant sailor and adventurer
Virginia Tilford: a wealthy woman of Providence
Nancy Kimble: her housekeeper

These characters should all be played in their upper thirties or early to late forties. It is important that Jack be old enough to have travelled the world a fair bit, and that Virginia's three happy years of marriage should have occurred when she was well into her twenties and able to command respect as an eminent hostess. One could make a case for playing Nancy either a bit younger or a bit older than the other two, but the intention is that she and Mrs. Tilford are contemporaries whose adventures allow them to transcend a barrier of social class.

S E T T I N G

The play takes place in Providence, Rhode Island in the summer of 1931.

As is evident from the listing of *Pith!*'s premiere production personnel, there were no designers for the play's set and lighting. This might not seem particularly odd for a Fringe production where the set must be put up in about fifteen minutes and struck in five, and lighting choices are often limited to what is available in a pre-existing hang. Although these limitations might normally seem to compromise a production, they actually help to clarify what is most important in *Pith!*: the performers are able to imagine and convey a journey of epic proportions through the simplest possible means. However, the production should not be stark. What few pieces there are onstage should be carefully chosen and warmly lit, but it is very important to avoid gilding this particular lily. The simpler everything is, the better the play will be, in fact the whole of the long scene at Virginia's must take place with the same light from beginning to end. All the jungle sounds should be generated by the actors with no other reinforcement. The only sound cues are the hymn in the church scene, the doorbell, and the recordings that play on the phonograph. It is also imperative that indicated Rosa Ponselle recordings are used. This voice is unique: Maria Callas or Renata Tebaldi just won't work in *Pith!*

Ponselle's arias are follows:

1) When Virginia is first seen she is listening to "O Nume Tutelar" from Spontini's *La Vestale*. The track starts as soon as the previous scene blacks out, and the lights are brought up on Virginia's room very slowly during the orchestral introduction, so the scene light is at full at about the same moment the voice is heard for the first time.

2) The recording Nancy plays to subdue the jungle creatures is "D'Amor Sul Ali Rosee" from Verdi's *Il Trovatore*. Jack and Nancy get particular mileage out of having their previously screechy forest voices attempt to gently echo the tops of the arching phrases.

3) Virginia's table setting ritual is performed to the "Ave Maria" from Verdi's *Otello*. Virginia stands still and listens for the first few lines of the prayer which are all on one note, and when the melody starts to expand she crosses to Nancy and collects the necessary items and begins. She has finished arranging things and is able to

fit her line, "Here is your grave . . ." into the short orchestral break near the end between "Ave Maria" and ". . . nell 'ora della morte." Then she touches everything for the last time and bows her head at the "Amen," as do Jack and Nancy. As the strings play out to the end, Virginia slowly rises, crosses to the phonograph, and lifts the needle just as the piece concludes.

4) "The Muskrat Ramble" was recorded by Louis Armstrong in the mid-1920s, and this is the preferred version for the play.

ACT ONE

Scene One
Jack Vail stands alone.

Jack: You've heard of Jack who was every inch a sailor. Well, that's not me. I'm the Jack who puts out to sea every now and again in search of a little peace and quiet, a change of scenery, and a few shekels. I'm Jack Vail, the potato peeler, the deck swabber, the freight handler, but never the sailor. A sailor loves the sea more than he loves the ports of call, and that's never been my way.

I'd been on a long haul, from Vera Cruz to New Orleans, then up the Eastern seaboard to Charleston and Savannah, till we finally put in at Providence, Rhode Island. Living in Providence for a while seemed like a good idea, so I installed myself in a rooming house, deposited my pay packet into a savings account, and set out to begin my providential existence. The first order of business was obvious. I went to church.

I don't consider myself a religious man, at least not in a specific, ecclesiastic sort of way. But spending a lot of time under the wide blue heavens on the great glassy sea can go a long way toward persuading a man of the existence of the Almighty, and so I do number myself among the faithful. More than anything, I'd say that after a few months in the exclusive company of coal-stokers and stevedores and the like, I crave the society of ladies and gentlemen together, and the eloquent communication which takes place in situations of moral constraint.

The first morning after my arrival in Providence was a Sunday, and so I headed for Saint Margaret's Presbyterian Church, where I'd been told the parishioners were most cordial and the congregational hymn singing was particularly enthusiastic. There were some benches at the back of the church and I chose to sit on one of those, in order to avoid usurping anyone's favourite pew. Just as the service was to begin I witnessed the arrival of a pair of extraordinary women who seated themselves directly across the aisle from me.

Jack has seated himself in a chair. As he speaks, Virginia Tilford and

Nancy Kimble enter and take their places opposite him.

Jack: The taller of them was extremely well dressed, with a very proud carriage. I sensed that she was a great beauty, though her face was obscured by the dark netting attached to her hat. Her companion, a shorter red-haired woman, was deferential in manner, and I thought immediately that she must be some sort of employee or servant. Unlike the dark lady, who murmured her responses and did not sing the hymns, the redhead was alert and attentive throughout and appeared moved by the proceedings. At the end of the service, the minister exhorted us to linger in the parish hall for a Pie Social and then there was a final hymn. It was a favourite of mine and I was happy to sing out.

A chorus swells. Jack and Nancy sing along enthusiastically. At the final word, the two women slip quickly away.

Jack: At the end of the recessional, I was surprised to note that the two women had slipped away. On reflection, it was easy to comprehend that the veiled lady wasn't exactly the pie noshing type. I myself like nothing more than a tasty wedge of blueberry or cherry pie and on this occasion I was able to sample both, while making the acquaintance of some charming Presbyterians. Having been told repeatedly that I must take a look at the fine colonial headstones in the churchyard cemetery, I finally slipped out of the hall to do just that. I was immediately startled to discover the mystery woman's red-haired companion, sitting by herself in the sunshine, eating a piece of bumbleberry pie . . . and crying.

Scene Two
Nancy sits on a little bench. She eats a piece of pie and occasionally dabs at her eyes with a handkerchief. Jack approaches and watches her for a moment.

Jack: Now, I hope those are tears of happiness you're shedding.

Nancy: Oh . . .What?

Jack: I thought the blueberry pie was a bit of heaven but I didn't weep when I tasted it. You're having the bumbleberry and it seems to be having an even more profound effect.

Nancy: Oh . . . no . . . I'm crying about . . . something else.

Jack: Then I'm sorry for disturbing you. I'll go back inside.

Nancy: No, you don't have to do that. I'll stop crying now and everything'll be fine.

Jack: You're sure?

Nancy: Oh yes.

She sobs involuntarily.

Jack: Oh-oh.

Nancy: I'm sorry. Now I'm embarrassed.

Jack: Why? Just because you're sad? You have a right to feel that way if you need to.

Nancy: But it's not appropriate here. The sun is shining, I've been to visit in God's House, and now I've got pie.

Jack: It wouldn't be the view of the cemetery that's pulling your spirits down?

Nancy: I don't think so. The graves are all about two hundred years old, so it doesn't usually depress me at all to be here. Does that make sense?

Jack: Sure. Here we are able to commune with the founders of Providence.

Nancy: Yes, that's right. I never thought to put it quite that way, but visiting this churchyard does usually put me in cheerful frame of mind. That's why I came out here when I felt myself being overcome by the weepies. And of course I didn't want to ruin the Pie Social for others by bursting into tears.

Jack: Well, one would hope their Presbyterian compassion might have overridden their need for carefree snacking, but I do understand your impulse. I think it shows generosity.

Nancy: You do?

Jack: Sure. But now I think you're owed something in return.

Nancy: Owed? By whom?

Jack: Well, on behalf of the other parishioners, I'd happily extend you some sort of courtesy. What would you like most right now? A fresh hankie? A shoulder to cry on? Another piece of pie?

Nancy: Oh no, thank you. None of those. Can I . . . Can I tell you why I'm sad?

Jack: Of course you can. But you'll have to do two other things first.

Nancy: Alright. What are they?

Jack: Number One: You'll have to tell me your name. Mine is Jack. Jack Vail.

Nancy: Mr. Vail, I'm Nancy Kimble.

Jack: *Shaking her hand.* Miss Kimble, I'm pleased to meet you.

Nancy: Likewise. And now, tell me the other thing I have to do.

Jack: Well . . . Before you tell me the reason for your unhappiness . . . I think you should cheer up. Then you'll have a little perspective.

Nancy: Well, Mr. Vail—

Jack:	Please . . . Jack.
Nancy:	Well Jack, that sounds like a good idea, but I'm not sure I know how to do it.
Jack:	Then I'll help you. Nancy, tell me a place you'd like to be. Where would you go on a holiday, if you could.
Nancy:	Oh, I'd probably take the day coach to Newport Beach. I've been there a few times and it's always pleasant.
Jack:	But now you can go anywhere. Anywhere in the world.
Nancy:	Oh, I don't know. I was at Cape Cod once when I was young, but that doesn't seem terribly original.
Jack:	You like the beach, Nancy?
Nancy:	I like the water and the sunshine.
Jack:	Then might I suggest Rio de Janeiro. How'd you like to go there?
Nancy:	Maybe I would. I've seen pictures. It looks gorgeous.
Jack:	Well then, I think you should close your eyes and bring those pictures to mind.
Nancy:	*Shuts her eyes.* Alright. Now they were black and white photos. Is that a problem?
Jack:	Why don't you shade them in. Pick the colours you like best.
Nancy:	Alright.
Jack:	And make them vivid. Bright reds and pinks and greens. Everything is vivid in Rio.
Nancy:	Yes, that's what I've heard.
Jack:	So, are you seeing it all now? Are you imagining yourself there?

Nancy:	I think I am.
Jack:	Are you on the beach?
Nancy:	Yes, I am. It's a beautiful crescent shaped beach. I feel the warm sand under my feet. And I look up and I see that huge rock with the statue on it and the mountain beside.
Jack:	Yes, that's Sugar Loaf Mountain.
Nancy:	But that's such a silly name for an important looking landmark.
Jack:	Well they don't want things to be too serious here. They want you to enjoy your holiday. Tell me Nancy, is the sun shining?
Nancy:	It certainly is. It's very bright, so it must be right around noon. I hope I don't burn.
Jack:	Maybe you won't if you don't want to.
Nancy:	I . . . What? Oh, yes. Would you look at that. I have a tan Jack. It's my first one ever. What a wonderful holiday I'm on.
Jack:	Are there a lot of other people on the beach?
Nancy:	A few. Just enough. I'm not in the middle of them. I have a little . . . what's that called . . . a little tent-hut thing . . .
Jack:	A cabana?
Nancy:	That's right. My cabana is right behind me.
Jack:	You must be close to the terrace of your hotel.
Nancy:	Oh, I am. You know . . . I can just hear a band playing. It's a little samba or something. Can you hear it?
Jack:	Sure I can. Nancy, have you ordered anything from the waiter?

Nancy:	Oh, I should, shouldn't I. That might put everything just so.
Jack:	He's coming along right now.
Nancy:	Oh yes. My, but he's a sleek specimen. Waiter, excuse me, waiter!
Jack:	Si, señorita . . . Ah, but what do I see? Are you not Nancy Kimble, the popular turista, this week's guest of honour here on the Copacabana?
Nancy:	Yes, that sounds like me.
Jack:	It is an honour to serve you today Señorita Kimble, for you are the kind of cool breeze who is always welcome in our sizzling town.
Nancy:	Oh please, I don't want to dampen the party down too much.
Jack:	I see no danger of that. From your fiery red hair I'd guess that you have a tempestuous side which will be unleashed as soon as night falls.
Nancy:	Yes, there's no telling what might happen when they play that Carioca.
Jack:	Ay yi yi, that's something to look forward to. But right now beautiful Rhode Island blossom, I have something special that you must taste. It is a rare and exotic pie. All the mysterious fruits of my country come together in mad conglomeration to tempt and tease you.
Nancy:	Oh, I must try this. I must have your pie, oh waiter of Brazil.
Jack:	Open your mouth then, and I will feed you a morsel.
Nancy:	Yes, please.

He gives her a forkful of pie.

Jack:	Is delectable? Yes? No?
Nancy:	It is! It is! It tastes a little like bumbleberry.
Jack:	But more vivid?
Nancy:	Yes yes. Everything is more vivid in Rio.
Jack:	And now Nancy, I'm afraid you must open your eyes and return to Providence. I'm thinking it's maybe not quite seemly for a gentleman to be feeding pie to a lady in the churchyard on a Sunday morning.
Nancy:	*Opens her eyes.* No, maybe not. Well, thank you for the holiday. It was just what I needed.
Jack:	And now you'll tell me why you're sad.
Nancy:	But I'm not sad. Not now. Maybe it'll all seem silly.
Jack:	And that wouldn't be such a bad end to things, would it?
Nancy:	No, you're right about that. So Jack, here it is. My employer is Mrs. Virginia Tilford. Perhaps you've heard of her?
Jack:	Actually, I haven't. I've only just come to town. I assume though, that she was the lady who sat next to you during the service.
Nancy:	Yes, that's right. You noticed us.
Jack:	I was just across the aisle from you, at the back. Mrs. Tilford cuts quite a striking figure.
Nancy:	She certainly does, but Jack, she'd never want to hear you say that. We attend church every Sunday, but we always sit at the back. We slip in at the last possible moment, and we always leave before the recessional hymn is done.
Jack:	She doesn't stay to socialize?

Nancy: Oh no, never. I don't usually either, even though she encourages me to. It's just too difficult, when I sense that people want to ask me about her. Well, not so much as they might have once, but . . . I'm getting ahead of myself. There was a time when Mrs. Tilford would have sat right up front and stayed afterward. She was a very prominent and popular hostess before . . . before her husband went away. She was very outgoing. She had many friends. Now it's different.

Jack: Her husband left her?

Nancy: Oh no, not like that. He went away and he didn't come back. Weldon Tilford was in silver. Silverware actually. The Tilfords have been in the business for over a hundred years. He went looking for of some kind of a mine in the middle of South America and was never heard from again.

Jack: How terrible. Did people search for him?

Nancy: To a certain extent, there were inquiries, but he had some sort of secret map and no one knew his actual destination, just that he was last seen in Ecuador.

Jack: And when was this?

Nancy: Nine, almost ten years ago.

Jack: And are there any theories at all about what may have happened?

Nancy: How can anyone know? He loved Mrs. Tilford very much, there was no doubt about that. They'd only been married three years and there's no way he'd have just run off and left her and his fortune and his business. So you see, that doesn't leave many options. It's very likely he's . . . She won't let us say it Jack. At first we all wanted to believe he'd turn up, so it was easy to keep hoping right along with her. But as the years went by, people just couldn't do it anymore. Even his family have accepted the likelihood of his not returning, so she won't speak to them at all.

There are legal matters to be dealt with . . . inheritances, insurance, bank accounts . . . but she won't let any of it happen. If anyone broaches the subject, she just stares them down like they're murderers.

Jack: When I saw the lady in church, I assumed she was a widow.

Nancy: She is a widow Jack. That's the first time I've said it and I'll probably never have another opportunity. She leads a widow's life, dressed in black, never going out. She's stored most of her nice things and she just sits in the dark with a few pieces of furniture, endlessly listening to her Rosa Ponselle records.

Jack: Well, it does sound like a sad situation. I suppose it's understandable that it might make you want to have a little cry.

Nancy: Well yes, but it was more specific than that. I just enjoyed the service so much today and so I stayed afterward and it was nice to be around all the people laughing and visiting . . . And I just realized that coming to the church every week gives us hope and so we celebrate that with our Pie Social, but Mrs. Tilford carries a different kind of hope inside her and she can't stand to be among the rest of us for fear that it might be extinguished. The irony of that made me sad, and then I thought maybe I'd never be able to come to another Pie Social because I'd always be too intensely aware of this unresolvable situation, and that's when I had to come out here.

Jack: Nancy, I'd like to help you.

Nancy: Jack, I think you already have in a way.

Jack: I'm sure I can do more for you, and for your employer too.

Nancy: But how?

Jack: The hope that Mrs. Tilford carries in her heart . . . I mean to extinguish it. To snuff it out.

Nancy:	You're very blunt Jack.
Jack:	I'm not. I can be pithy when the occasion demands.
Nancy:	How's that?
Jack:	I'm inclined to want to get to the heart of things quickly.
Nancy:	You're a practical man?
Jack:	I can be. But Nancy, pith and practicality don't necessarily preclude a life of adventure.
Nancy:	I don't know what you're talking about.
Jack:	Tomorrow all will be clear. If you'll write down your address for me, I'll call on Mrs. Tilford in the afternoon and take care of this matter.
Nancy:	I can't imagine what you'll do. Should I tell her you're coming?
Jack:	Absolutely not. The element of surprise is key here, and the first thing I'll do when I arrive will be to put her right off balance. Not physically though. *Taps his forehead.* Here.
Nancy:	Jack, I'm not sure I should know any more.
Jack:	Just as well, since I haven't quite imagined all the details. Nancy, I must go and prepare. *Takes the paper from her.* Thanks. It has been a true pleasure to share this time and pie with you.
Nancy:	Yes, thank you. I'll see you tomorrow . . . When?
Jack:	Around one o'clock. Goodbye Nancy.
Nancy:	Goodbye Jack.

He exits. She looks bemused, then finishes her pie.

Scene Three

In Virginia Tilford's sitting room, the following day. There are four chairs, very formally arranged, a small coffee table and a muted Persian carpet. Virginia sits in one chair, doing needlepoint. The sombre voice of Rosa Ponselle in Spontini's La Vestale is heard emanating from a phonograph in one corner. After a while, Virginia gets up and shuts off the record, then returns to her seat and resumes her needlework. Nancy enters.

Nancy: Oh, you are in here.

Virginia: Yes.

Nancy: It's so quiet. Do you want me to turn over the record?

Virginia: Thank you Nancy, but I shut it off. The music was depressing me a little.

Nancy: Doesn't it always? With all due respect Mrs. Tilford, I think a steady diet of Madame Ponselle's singing can't be good for anybody.

Virginia: Not so. There is no greater singer. Her artistry almost always lifts my spirits.

Nancy: Really? She has pretty much the reverse effect on me.

Virginia: Perhaps you are confusing spiritual exaltation with cheerfulness.

Nancy: Maybe.

Virginia: It doesn't matter. Today, the music came to my ears from some imperceptibly altered angle and failed to have its intended effect. The fault is not Ponselle's and if blame must be assigned, I will accept it.

Nancy: You know, I have a number of peppier items in my own collection. I could bring down—

Virginia: No thank you Nancy. Silence is what I am preferring today.

Nancy: Very well. I've cleared away the lunch things. Will you want tea later?

Virginia: I expect I will. What time is it now?

The doorbell chimes. Nancy smiles.

Nancy: It must be one o'clock.

Virginia: Who can that be? I'm not expecting anyone.

Nancy: I'll go and see.

Virginia: Use discretion Nancy. I may not be at home.

Nancy: Of course.

She exits. Virginia puts aside her needlework and paces, clearly put out. Nancy returns.

Nancy: There's a gentleman here who's asking to see you. He says he's a Government Adjuster.

Virginia: Oh, for heaven's sake, why wouldn't he make an appointment?

Nancy: He says his business will only take a few moments. Shall I let him in?

Virginia: I suppose you should. But Nancy, stay with us and be prepared to escort him out if I should suddenly excuse myself.

Nancy: Of course.

Nancy exits. Virginia returns to her chair and sits stiffly. After a moment Nancy enters with Jack. He carries a small suitcase which he leaves by the entrance.

Nancy: Mrs. Tilford, Mr. Vail is here.

Virginia: Good afternoon sir.

Jack: Mrs. Tilford, thank you for seeing me. May I sit?

Virginia: Yes.

Jack: *Sits across from her.* Mrs. Tilford, I am a representative of the United States Government. I am an Adjuster.

Virginia: Yes, so Nancy has told me, and though I'm not certain just what exactly that means, I can guess that it has to do with the usual matters of inheritance and insurance which are the bane of my existence. So I'll save us both some time Mr. Vail, by reiterating right here and now what I've said to all who've approached me on this tiresome business over the years and this is that my husband is missing. His absence, however protracted cannot be taken as definite proof that he is decea—

Jack: Oh, Mrs. Tilford, I must stop you right there, for my business with you is far from personal. I have come to adjust your furniture.

Virginia: I beg your pardon?

Jack: My branch of the government has been doing specialized secret research for a number of years. Very secret. Very unknown. A clandestine operation, not subversive, but certainly . . . shhh. And our findings have been considerable and significant. It may be that all of the people of the Americas will lead better lives because of what we've discovered. Isn't that wonderful Mrs. Tilford?

Virginia: I . . . Yes.

Jack: We are implementing right now a sort of a test program here in Providence and—

Virginia: A moment please. Are you about to ask me for money?

Jack: *Stands.* Mrs. Tilford, I am wounded by that. I certainly am not going to ask you for money. The government has plenty.

Virginia: Forgive me. I've been preyed on before.

Jack: No no, the fault is mine, for not hurrying to the point. Here it comes now. Have you heard of ions, Mrs. Tilford?

Virginia: I suppose I have. They're some kind of tiny particles, aren't they?

Jack: Oh yes, tiny is what they are, but sig-nificant. They are electrically charged atoms and they are all around us. They are in the air we breathe, so you can imagine what that means.

Virginia: Actually, I can't.

Jack: They are inside us. *Inhales.* You see? Ions rush in. *Exhales.* And out. I'm an active man Mrs. Tilford. That means I breathe a good deal. Ions are always going to be a part of me. What I've realized is that they must be kept happy.

Virginia: Happy? You mean . . . content?

Jack: Why yes, I do. Does it surprise you to realize that these tiny electrified particles might have an emotional life?

Virginia: Well, I—

Jack: Think of it. Electrification, kineticism. Do these things not imply a capacity for spontaneous feeling? Why am I asking you? I'm the expert. Sorry to patronize, and here's the answer. Yes. The ion is wildly emotional.

Nancy covers her mouth and looks from side to side nervously.

Jack: And like many who might be described in this way, they are free-spirited and given to endless random movement. Ions, Mrs. Tilford, are the little gypsies of the particulate world. *He pauses and looks away.*

Virginia: Don't stop now Mr. Vail.

Jack: Oh, I won't. But I pause, for I've reached the point where

I must reveal a discovered truth which never fails to startle and unsettle persons like ourselves who've been raised to believe that we've the right, based on our intelligence, to set forth the elements of our environment in the way that best pleases us. Mrs. Tilford, we are wrong in that assumption.

Virginia: Oh?

Jack: I'm going to be intensely specific now.

Virginia: Good.

Jack: The arrangement of furniture in the modern world is ruining life for the ions. And the problem is most particular in the homes of well-to-do citizens like yourself, who lean toward the formal. Right angles, that's what's doing it. The ions are being channelled, and this is making them annoyed. Their electrical charges increase and as we are bombarded by them repeatedly in the same places, we are rendered forgetful or irritable or emotionally numb. Look at the chairs in your sitting room, Mrs. Tilford, all set neatly around the edge of the carpet. Why is this so?

Virginia: I just like the—

Jack: I'm sorry, I don't know why I keep asking you questions when it's obvious I have a specific agenda to press. I won't waste your time. That isn't the point of my visit. It is obvious to me that you have arranged your furniture according to the Arcadian, Palladian, rules of classical symmetry, under the assumption that this will promote a sense of tranquillity and order in your room. But now we know what a mistake this is. Mrs. Tilford, tell me . . . Are you . . . No, sorry. Mrs. Tilford, you are not happy. That's apparent. And so to remedy this situation—

Virginia: *Rises.* Mr. Vail, I must ask you to leave my home at once.

Jack: You can't do that. I work for the government. I can just get an order allowing me to conduct my business—

Virginia:	Well, what exactly is your business here, Mr. Vail?
Jack:	I'm here to adjust the furniture. I said that before.
Virginia:	But what did you mean?
Jack:	I just move it. Like this. *He crosses to a pair of neatly arranged chairs and turns them at odd angles.* There, you see? That's a start. You won't feel a difference right away but—
Virginia:	This is preposterous. I can't have a room that looks like this.
Jack:	You'll get used to it. Others have.
Virginia:	*Sits in a chair.* I can't imagine how. What happens when I have a guest?
Jack:	*Sits in a chair which faces another direction.* He sits here. Perhaps you raise your voices a little. *Twists.* Or you may investigate different physical positions which may actually add to the piquancy of your communication. *He is leaning on one elbow, looking over his shoulder.* You see? Saucy. Perhaps not appropriate just now, but a whole range of options will open up. Miss Kimble, if you will . . . *He indicates a chair and Nancy comes forward and sits in it. He sets his chair directly across from hers.* Here is how things have gone before. Miss Kimble, how do you do?
Nancy:	Very well. Thank you for asking.
Jack:	Have you read any good novels lately?
Nancy:	Not really. I prefer the movies. I saw a good one last week, but I forget what it was called.
Jack:	Aha, you see. Forgetfulness, brought on by ionic bombardment. Now, Miss Kimble . . . May I call you Nancy?
Virginia:	How do you know her name?

Jack: I am a government agent, Mrs. Tilford. I know . . . much.
           Nancy, let's move your chair over here and put mine . . .
           here. *He places the chairs beside each other, but facing in dif-
           ferent directions.*

Jack: Now we try again.

They sit.

Jack: Nancy, how are you doing?

Nancy: Oh, very well. Thank you for asking.

Jack: Have you seen any good movies lately?

Nancy: Yes, I have actually. And the best one was called *Make Way
           for Tomorrow.*

Jack: Ah, you see. Progress already.

Virginia: That's ridiculous. She just had time to think.

Jack: Oh maybe, but the thing of it is that we can be much more
           relaxed because we don't have to face each other. Our con-
           versation doesn't turn into an interview, something that
           too often happens in the standard drawing room setting,
           with its preponderance of opportunities for eye contact.

Virginia: Isn't eye contact a good thing? Is it not the hallmark of
           sincere communication?

Jack: I think it's been overused. Its power is diluted.

Virginia: Does this have anything to do with the ions?

Jack: How could it not?

Virginia: What?

Jack: Exactly. What? What do you think?

Virginia: I thought you were going to stop asking me questions.

Jack: Maybe I'd stop if I couldn't see you.

Virginia: Alright.

She moves a chair and sits in it so he can't see her from his chair.

Jack: Mrs. Tilford, it's thrilling for me to have you embrace the principles of my research.

Virginia: *Faces upstage.* I have never been more miserable than I am at this moment. Mr. Vail, you've made a fool of me, and what's more, you've made a fool of my home.

Jack: How can I convince you, dear lady, that your unease is caused by a lifetime of enslavement to the principle of—

Virginia: *Rises and turns.* No! I've endured ten years on the lip of despair and it has nothing to do with my furniture. Mr. Vail, you say that you know much, so you must be aware that my husband disappeared in a remote and inhospitable corner of the world. I carry a core of uncertainty in me, a huge gaping hole in the centre of my being and if I have to live with something like that, I'm going to have my chairs neatly placed, no matter what it does to your little electrified particles.

Jack: *Shakes his head.* Oh, Mrs. Tilford, I am sorry. I am very sorry for your . . . for you. Clearly the situation that exists in this household is not amenable to the swift implementation of my precepts and findings. Dear dear dear.

Virginia: I'd have thought, Mr. Vail, that having reached that conclusion, you'd be moved to excuse yourself from my home.

Jack: Please, Mrs. Tilford. I am thinking. I am thinking as I've never thought before.

Virginia: Well, I've no inclination to watch this. I am going upstairs to lie on my bed, which has an agreeably perpendicular relationship with the walls of my room. Nancy, please show Mr. Vail out when the opportunity presents itself. Sooner, if you prefer.

Jack: Mrs. Tilford. Please stay. I implore you!

Virginia: Sir, you're an uninvited guest in my home. I can only marvel that you'd think it appropriate to implore me to remain in a room with you.

Jack: Nevertheless, I have, and I've also turned to face you as a means of adding sincerity to the mix. Mrs. Tilford, I want to help you.

Virginia: With what?

Jack: Why, with your uncertainty. With that thing that is eating away at you from the inside.

Virginia: Mr. Vail, I was frank with you because I wanted you to leave me alone, not because I wanted your help and sympathy.

Jack: But the solution to your troubles is so simple and clear.

Virginia: Is it?

Jack: Yes. You must go in search of your husband. You must find out what happened to him and you must set all of your doubts and fears to rest.

Virginia: God help us, Nancy. He's a madman!

Jack: I'm not! Tell me Mrs. Tilford, haven't you often wished that you could just set out for the wilds of South America, a forthright adventuress on a quest?

They stare at each other in silence for a moment.

Jack: You don't have to say anything, because the answer is clear.

Virginia: Of course I've considered it, Mr. Vail. In ten years of applied brooding, how could I not? But I cannot begin to imagine how I would go about undertaking such a journey.

Jack: I should think that imagining it might be the best and easiest way to begin.

Virginia: As usual, I don't understand you.

Jack: Well Let's take action and clarify things then.

He sets two pairs of chairs opposite each other.

Virginia: This is only a dream. It's a nightmare and soon I'll be awake.

Jack: Well, if that's the case, then we've no time to lose. Mrs. Tilford, may I ask you to sit here, and Miss Kimble, here.

Nancy sits.

Virginia: May I ask w—

Jack: Of course I'm going to tell you. Please sit.

She sits.

Jack: You are on a train bound for New Orleans. There you'll depart on your ocean voyage to South America. You are accompanied by the devoted Nancy Kimble.

Virginia: This is such nonsense.

Nancy: No it isn't Mrs. Tilford. We have to do what he says.

Virginia: Nancy?

Nancy: I just . . . I just trust Mr. Vail, for no apparent reason. You should too.

Virginia: Well, I don't see how I can argue with that kind of logic so . . . Alright, we're on a train. Is it moving?

Jack: Oh yes. You've just pulled out of the station.

Nancy: Oh . . . then . . . *She starts to jiggle in her seat.*

Virginia: Nancy, what on earth are you doing?

Nancy: I'm jiggling with the movement of the train.

Virginia: We're in first class, so the suspension is excellent. Stop it.

Nancy stops jiggling. Virginia turns to Jack.

Virginia: Who are you? Are you the conductor?

Jack: Yes, exactly. May I see your tickets please?

Virginia: Nancy, give him the tickets.

Nancy: *Flustered.* Oh, I . . . they may be in the luggage.

Jack: Please, don't worry about it. I can check them later at your convenience. Mrs. Tilford, it's an honour to have you on board.

Virginia: You know me? That's reassuring.

Jack: Ah yes. We're all aware of your quest to the Southern Hemisphere. On behalf of all who travel, I wish you well.

Virginia: I wasn't aware word had gotten out so quickly. I feel as though I've hardly had time to formulate my plan.

Jack: Well if I can be of assistance in this or any other matter, please don't hesitate to ring for me.

Virginia: Certainly, I will. Nancy, give the man a gratuity.

Nancy: Oh . . . yes. *Extends a sideways palm.* Here you are porter.

Virginia: He's the conductor.

Jack: Oh, what's in a name. *Takes the imaginary coin.* Thank you very much.

They nod. He withdraws.

Virginia:	Nancy, you're going to have to calm down a little. We're only on the first leg of a very long journey.
Nancy:	I'm sorry Mrs. Tilford. It's just that we're an hour out of the station and already I'm farther from home than I've ever been in my life.
Virginia:	Well we mustn't be frightened. We've a serious purpose and we must keep our wits about us. Also the weather is lovely where we're headed and I see no reason why we can't relax a bit. After all, I've spent the last ten years in self-inflicted gloom.
Nancy:	That's very candid of you ma'am.
Virginia:	I suppose it is. But Nancy, on holiday one may surprise oneself.
Nancy:	I'm excited to hear that. I only hope I bear up well in the hot weather. I hear the sun comes very near the earth, down Ecuador way.
Virginia:	Yes, well you can't— . . . *She stops for a moment, then covers her face with her hands.* This is wrong. This is terribly wrong.

She gets up and crosses away. She stands with her back to Jack and Nancy for a moment, then hurries out. Nancy and Jack slowly turn to one another.

Nancy:	Oh dear. Jack, I thought we were doing so well.
Jack:	Yes, I did too.
Nancy:	Do you think . . . Are we out of luck now?
Jack:	I'm afraid it's quite possible, and that's too bad. We had her defences right down and she was thoroughly confused about the furniture.
Nancy:	Just like I was. I wish I'd known what exactly you were working toward. Then I could have been more help.

Jack: Oh, don't blame yourself. It's my fault for just trying to wing it.

Nancy: Do you think there's any point in trying to carry on, or come at this from some other side?

Jack: I really doubt that we could. We'll have lost the element of surprise, and now Nancy, I'm afraid I'll have pushed her into some darker and more brooding place than she was in before.

Nancy: Don't be blaming yourself Jack. She perpetuates it on her own and she's as much as admitted it.

Jack: All the same, it's not going to make your life much easier.

Nancy: Oh, I'll manage. It's not like she knows I had anything to do with this.

Jack: I suppose I'll just set this furniture back where it belongs and I'll be on my way.

Nancy: Yes, I guess that's best.

They set about putting the chairs in the same prim order they were in previously.

Jack: There. Just as it was.

Nancy: These chairs are going to make me nervous. All the little ions whizzing around. Is there any truth to any of that?

Jack: I don't see why there couldn't be.

Nancy: So, what have you got in that suitcase?

Jack: I brought a number of hats. Scarves, paraphernalia . . . Oh well.

Nancy: Jack, I'm grateful to you. I don't quite know how to—

Jack: Please, Nancy, I didn't do anything.

Nancy: Oh, but you did. Yesterday, and today, you . . . Jack, you . . .

He smiles. He places one hand on her cheek and they look at each other for a moment. Virginia sweeps into the room, now wearing a tan coloured travelling ensemble and carrying a straw travel bag. Nancy breaks away from Jack with a gasp.

Nancy: Mrs. Tilford . . . You've changed.

Virginia: Of course I have. I don't know what I was thinking, heading out for a tropical climate in black crepe. This is much more suitable. And who is the gentleman please?

Jack: *Southern.* Mrs. Tilford, my name is Sanborn Preflax. I have to come to extend you an official welcome from the City of New Orleans.

Virginia: Have you? Well Mr. Preflax, I'm very honoured, and I'm only curious as to why you had your hand on the face of my amanuensis.

Jack: Nothing untoward, I assure you ma'am. Miss Kimble had a sudden reaction to the Louisiana climate and asked me for an objective assessment of her body temperature.

Virginia: *Hands Nancy her travel bag.* Nancy, you must be careful not to overexert yourself. Now Mr. Preflax, touched as I am by your welcome, I must tell you that we've only a few hours before our ship sails for the equatorial regions. Have we anything further to discuss?

Jack: Mrs. Tilford, I confess I did jockey very deliberately to be chosen to greet you. I have something to impart to you which may be of value on your quest.

Virginia: Well then, we must find somewhere we can speak privately.

Jack: Of course. May I recommend the terrace of the Hotel Excelsior?

Virginia: That sounds quite acceptable. Is it nearby?

Jack: Yes, very near. *Gestures at Nancy.* We are almost upon it.

Nancy scurries to set up a pair of chairs.

Jack: Yes, here we are. Shall we sit?

Virginia: Yes. My word, these rattan chairs are impressive. It's hard
             to believe I'm still in my own country.
They sit.

Jack: Will you have something to drink Mrs. Tilford?

Virginia: Yes, that would be delightful.

Jack: Service can be a little slow out here. Perhaps—

Virginia: Nancy, why don't you go in search of some cocktails for
             us.

Nancy: Yes, of course. Anything in particular?

Jack: I recommend the Rickeys.

Virginia: Perfect. A pair of Rickeys, Nancy.

Nancy: Yes ma'am.

She exits.

Virginia: So Mr. Preflax, what is it we must discuss?

Jack: Mrs. Tilford, I knew your husband.

Virginia: Oh, did you?

Jack: Yes. We had business dealings.

Virginia: I see. Are you also in the silver trade?

Jack: No no. My dealings are many and various. I'm what you
             might call . . . a trader of information.

Virginia:	That sounds euphemistic, Mr. Preflax. Are you a bad man?
Jack:	I don't think that's for me to say, finally.
Virginia:	Perhaps not. So, you say you knew my husband?
Jack:	Yes, though we met only twice. Once, when I made him a proposal, and the second time when we closed our deal.
Virginia:	And what was the nature of this deal, Mr. Preflax?
Jack:	I sold your husband a map disclosing the location of an unclaimed cachet of silver in the Orienté region of Ecuador.
Virginia:	I see. For ten years myself and others have wondered just what led him to this remote region. Now I find it was you.
Jack:	Yes. I fear you'll be angry with me. You'll hold me responsible.
Virginia:	My husband was an enterprising businessman Mr. Preflax. He went where he pleased and nothing that happened to him could ever be considered your fault.
Jack:	You're kind to say so.
Virginia:	I wonder though, how exactly this map came to be in your possession?
Jack:	Mrs. Tilford, there are certain secrets of my trade which I cannot divulge.
Virginia:	Of course. Can you tell me though, why you wouldn't go after the treasure yourself?
Jack:	*Aging a little.* I'm not a young man Mrs. Tilford.
Virginia:	Aren't you? I hadn't realized.
Jack:	I'm comfortably well off and I've no need to exert myself in pursuit of a fortune.

Virginia: I see. Especially when there's a good chance that that fortune's existence may prove to be apocryphal?

Jack: Mrs. Tilford, I—

Virginia: I think you **are** a bad man Mr. Preflax.

Jack: Ah well, you're not the first to say so.

Virginia: So why is it you wanted to talk to me? The information you've offered so far seems quite useless.

Jack: Mrs. Tilford, I have something else for you.

Virginia: Something for sale?

Jack: I should say so. I am an enterprising businessman after all, and I know that's something you respect.

Virginia: Yes, and what is it you'd like me to buy from you?

Jack: I made a copy . . . one single copy . . . of the map I sold your husband. *Takes out a folded piece of paper.* This is it.

Virginia: I see. And what would be the figure you're seeking in exchange for this document?

He takes out a small pad and pencil, jots down a figure and shows it to her.

Virginia: That's expensive, but obviously the information is well worth it.

She takes a chequebook from her bag, writes a cheque, and hands it to him. He hands her the map.

Jack: Thank you. That was easy. But you haven't written in my name, Mrs. Tilford.

Virginia: No, I haven't. Mr. Preflax, my husband is still officially classified as a missing person. The information you've offered regarding his whereabouts should really have been made available ten years ago, and your offering of it now in exchange for money seems to me both imprudent and possibly felonious. I feel I may have a responsibility to report you to the Federal Bureau of Investigation, but I'm in a hurry, so if you were to make that cheque payable to one of the finer children's hospitals of New Orleans, I might manage to overlook the whole matter.

They stare at one another for a moment. Nancy enters with two cocktails on a tray.

Nancy: Here we are. Rickeys for two.

Virginia: Thank you Nancy. *She takes a cocktail and drains it at a gulp.* Well that was bracing. Just the thing on a hot day. Mr. Preflax, I'm sure you'll enjoy yours. *She takes the other drink and tosses it in Jack's face.* Come Nancy, we must board our vessel.

She walks off and stands with her back to the others. Nancy looks at Jack with concern, but he gestures that all's well and crosses upstage wiping his face with a handkerchief. Virginia turns to Nancy.

Virginia: *Breathes in sharply.* Ah Nancy, is there anything more invigorating than the start of an ocean voyage?

Nancy: Uhh . . . No ma'am. I don't expect there is.

Virginia leads Nancy briskly downstage.

Virginia: But here we are, nine days out at sea and it just seems so tiresome. The Gulf of Mexico, the Pacific Ocean . . .Who'd have thought they'd look so much alike.

Nancy: Yes, water's water, any way you look at it I guess.

Virginia: I wonder how long it is till lunch is served. Not for hours I expect. However will we pass the time?

Nancy: I don't know. Shuffleboard?

Virginia: Ah yes, inevitably there's that. But it never was my game, even when I was young and still subject to the competitive urge. I suppose we might just as well sit in our deck chairs and take advantage of the ever-increasing proximity of the sun.

They sit.

Virginia: Now Nancy, do you see that gentleman over there?

Nancy: Looks at Jack. Right there?

Virginia: Yes yes, but don't draw attention to us looking at him. That man has been following me rather closely ever since he boarded at Panama.

Nancy: Should we be alarmed?

Virginia: I think maybe not. He seems to be more concerned with getting himself noticed than the opposite, so I think he's perhaps a fortune hunter of the least harmful variety. What do you think of his looks?

Nancy: Nice enough. Maybe a little oily, but then so is a lot of the food in these climates.

Virginia: Nancy, I think we ought to have a little fun with him.

Nancy: Oh?

She whispers a few words to Nancy, who giggles, nods, and exits quickly. During their conversation, Jack has altered his stance and appearance, and now saunters over with the practiced slouch of the gigolo.

Virginia: *Smiles.* Good day Señor.

Jack: Ah, at long last the beautiful Americana favours me with a greeting.

Virginia: Alas, I've been feeling a little shy. But I've got my sea-legs now and the confidence that goes with them, so I've resolved to get to know some of my fellow passengers.

Jack: And am I the first?

Virginia:	Indeed you are. I wonder what your name might be.
Jack:	I am Robleto Maranón.
Virginia:	Ah yes, like the River Maranón which feeds the great Amazon.
Jack:	The lady knows her geography.
Virginia:	I've had cause to study a few maps.
Jack:	Of course you have, for you are the valiant and questing Mrs. Tilford.
Virginia:	Yes yes, that's me.
Jack:	Señora, if there's any way I might be of service to you while we are on board this ship, please let me know what it is. It troubles me to see a lady such as yourself travelling unescorted.
Virginia:	Oh, but I feel quite safe. I'm certain that—
Jack:	*Falls on one knee.* Mrs. Tilford, I must speak honestly. You are so beautiful and courageous. I find that I cannot help being in love with you. It is foolish, I know, for you are a great and wealthy—
Virginia:	Robleto, please. I must confess something to you before you go any further. I am not who you think I am. My name is Nancy Kimble. My employer and I exchanged identities on this voyage for the sake of her safety. I'm afraid I'm only a poor housekeeper, but if you still find me—

Nancy enters with some phonograph recordings.

Jack:	Leaps up and crosses to her. Señora, I must tell you, if there is any way I can be of service to you—
Nancy:	*Quickly puts down the records.* I beg your pardon sir?
Virginia:	Oh Mrs. Tilford, I'm afraid I've spilled the beans to this man.

Nancy: I see. Because he looked so trustworthy?

Virginia: How ashamed I am now.

Nancy: So what's your hash there Pedro?

Jack: I am Robleto Maranón, at your service.

Nancy: At my service? Really?

Jack: Yes, of course. For you are beautiful and courageous and I find that—

Nancy: Whoa there amigo, no need to lay it on too thick. I'm a high-class dame and I've heard this song before.

Jack: Ah, you wound me with your implication.

Nancy: Ooops, sorry. Well, as long as you've declared yourself, how's about you escort me to the tea dance on the poop deck.

Jack: It would be an honour.

Nancy: *Takes his arm.* Great. It's just this way. And here we are. The band should be starting at any moment.

Virginia has crossed to the phonograph and is putting on a record.

Jack: I am excited. In my toes, there is a tingling.

Nancy: Ah, a tingling for the tango perhaps?

Jack: We can only hope, Señora Tilford.

The music starts. It is emphatically not a tango.

Nancy: Ah, it's the "Muskrat Ramble." Well, I like that one too. *She leads him in a slightly frenetic dance.* Say, you're not half bad at this. You must have Rambled before.

Jack: I may have.

Nancy: Well, I suppose a man in your line of work ought to know his way around the dance floor.

Jack: Señora, I don't understand you.

Nancy: No? Must be my Spanish. I apologize.

They dance some more. He propels her in a spin, then they abruptly reverse and turn in the opposite direction.

Nancy: Say, now I'm leading. How did that happen?

Jack: We've just crossed the equator. Now things turn in reverse.

Nancy: Oh my.

Virginia: *Approaches.* I'm bored. May I cut in?

Jack: *To Nancy.* Mrs. Tilford?

Nancy: Oh, by all means.

She breaks away from Jack and starts dancing with Virginia. They finish and applaud one another and the band.

Virginia: Oh Nancy, what fun! I haven't danced like that in years.

Nancy: I'm happy to hear it, but maybe you're a little disoriented. You just called me Nancy and that's your name.

Virginia: Oh, I'm a silly.

Jack: Something is wrong. I suspect female treachery. Am I deceived?

Nancy: Maybe you are. And it would just serve you right there, Pancho.

Jack: I don't know what you mean.

Nancy: My watch. It was here on my wrist and now it's not.

Jack: I'm sure I've no—

Nancy: Would you please empty your jacket pocket sir.

Jack: Of course. *He reaches into a pocket and pulls out Nancy's watch, which she herself has put there while they were dancing.* What the . . .

Virginia: Aha! Nancy, you have caught him out.

Jack: Nancy, Nancy! Which of you is the real Nancy?

Nancy: Oh Robleto, does it matter?

Jack: No, I suppose it doesn't. I am exposed and so I must leave the ship. Adios ladies, it was a delightful afternoon.

He slips off his shoes and sets them aside. He puts two chairs together and steps up onto them. He crosses himself, plugs his nose and leaps over the backs.

Virginia: My word, Nancy, he's leapt overboard. He'll certainly drown.

Nancy: *Looks over the edge.* I don't know if that's so Mrs. Tilford. If what they say about oil and water is true, then I don't think he'll be sinking anytime soon. Anyhow, we don't have time to worry about him. We've crossed the equator and that means we're almost ready to land. We'd best prepare to disembark. I wonder what sort of port we're getting off at.

Virginia: *Looks at her map.* It doesn't matter, for we must head inland as quickly as possible, through the highlands and into the jungles of Orienté.

Nancy: How will we do that?

Virginia: On the train, I'd imagine.

Nancy: Yes, of course. *She hurries to set up another train compartment with facing chairs.* I believe this is our coach here.

Virginia: Really? Well I guess there was no reason to expect comfort here in the middle of nowhere.

Nancy: At least the weather is nice.

They sit in their seats.

Nancy: I hope the suspension is as good as on our American trains.

Virginia: *Jiggles violently.* I wouldn't count on it.

Nancy: *Jiggles.* Oh dear. I hope it's not a long journey.

Jack: *Approaches, jiggling also.* Ladies, good day.

Virginia: Good day. Are you the conductor?

Jack: No, not at all. I am Count Alfred Popping, the Swedish geologist.

Virginia: Oh Count, forgive me. I'm rattled by the poor suspension and the equatorial glare.

Jack: It's nothing Madame, I assure you. May I sit in your compartment for a little?

Virginia: Please. Allow me to introduce myself. I am Mrs. Virginia Tilford and this is Miss Nancy Kimble.

Jack: Mrs. Tilford, Miss Kimble. May a fellow inquire as to what brings an elegant pair like yourselves to undertake a daunting inland journey in this treacherous republic?

Virginia: We are searching for a missing person.

Jack: Ah, of course. That is a popular activity among travellers in these lower Americas.

Virginia: Count Popping, did I hear you correctly. Are you a geologist?

Jack:	Yes, that's right. I'm a geologist and a nobleman. How times have changed, eh? Hah hah hah!
Virginia:	Perhaps you'll be able to advise us. We are seeking not only a missing person, but also a legendary cachet of silver in the region called Orienté.
Jack:	Silver, you say? A silver mine in the jungle? What are the chances of that? Silver ought to be in the mountains, or at least the highlands, wouldn't you think?
Virginia:	But I have a map. You see?
Jack:	Studies her map. Well, yes, but that doesn't make it any more likely. A silver mine in the jungle? What a funny idea to have! Hah hah hah!
Nancy:	If you please Count, Mrs. Tilford's husband disappeared in search of that mine. We take its existence very seriously.
Jack:	Forgive me, but I think your quest is folly. Pure folly. You'll never succeed. You may well be doomed. Hah hah. Yes, doomed.
Nancy:	Yeah, well, that's your opinion.
Jack:	It certainly is, and it's got to be right for I am a geologist and a man. Hah hah hah. Still, a difference of opinion doesn't mean we can't enjoy our trip together. Shall I ring for the porter and order a bottle of something nice. The local wine is delicious, made from bananas . . .
Virginia:	No, thank you. And perhaps this is our stop we're approaching.
Jack:	Ah, no it certainly isn't. I'll be getting off here, while you must carry on into the dense and uncharted lands of eastern Ecuador. Goodbye ladies. I wish you as much luck as you can possibly find. You'll need it, certainly and—
Nancy:	Oh just scram, ya nitwit!

He goes off.

Virginia: Nancy, let's never be as vulgar as the surroundings.

Nancy: I can't help it. That was the first man we've met who hasn't tried to defraud you, and I still liked him the least.

Virginia: We must expect to have our steadfastness tested with ever-increasing regularity as we approach the most challenging part of our quest.

Nancy: Oh dear. Perhaps we should have got some of that banana wine, just for fortitude.

Virginia: No Nancy. Our strength must be the genuine article.

Nancy: *Sighs.* Well, I'll see what I can muster.

Virginia: Look here. The formidable River Napo. We must navigate its waters inland, for there are no longer any roads or train tracks.

Nancy: But how—

Virginia: We'll hire a boat and a little man to row it. Excuse me . . . Holla, You there, Inca!

Jack scurries over. He looks at Virginia suspiciously out of one eye.

Virginia: Is that your boat tethered there?

Jack squawks affirmatively.

Virginia: We would like to hire you for a river voyage. Is that possible?

He mutters uncomprehendingly.

Virginia: Nancy, I don't know how to communicate with this gentleman.

Nancy: *Gesticulates wildly.* You takie me and her . . . in boat . . . paddle paddle paddle . . . far far far . . . Got money. Yes?

Jack: *Laughs.* Ka ka ka ka!

Nancy: I think he's interested.

Jack babbles frantically, gesturing to convey a question of distance.

Nancy: I . . . I . . . I think he wants to know how far we're going.

Virginia: *Looks at her map.* Well, let's see . . . To Chimpiquetlixotle. At least that far.

Jack: Ayiyiyiyiyi! *He shakes his head and makes the evil eye.*

Nancy: Oh oh. Not a favoured destination.

Virginia: Nancy, give him your watch.

Nancy: But . . .

Virginia: I'll buy you a new one.

Nancy: Hmm . . . *Hands the watch to Jack.* Here. What do you say?

Jack: Okee dokee.

He moves the chairs and creates a small rowboat. The ladies climb aboard rather gingerly.

Jack: *Provides each of the ladies with a pith helmet.* Eh? Eh?

Virginia: Oh. Thank you.

Nancy: Say, now we can face the unknown in style.

Virginia: Nancy, how do I look?

Nancy: Superb, Mrs. Tilford. Now you have dash.

Virginia: I feel outrageous. Thank heavens there's no one around to see.

Nancy: Yes, they've certainly got peace and quiet to spare down here.

They relax and recline in the boat. Jack is kneeling behind them, paddling slowly.

Virginia: I can't say I'm at peace. Not yet. But for now this is soothing. All those years I spent quietly in the dark and yet I was restless and perturbed. Now I'm assaulted on all sides by strange sights and sounds and I find myself beginning to relax.

Nancy: It's too bad our steersman can't supply us with a little information about where we are and what goes on here.

They look at him, then smile and shrug.

Jack: *Speaks rapidly, without an accent.* The boundaries of the Orienté region have never been clearly defined, and this has led to constant disputes between the people of Ecuador and their neighbours in Colombia, Peru, and Brazil. In this largely unexplored rain forest area, one may find rubber, camphor, vanilla, sarsaparilla, as well as ipecac, the creeping plant whose roots, when dried, can be used quite effectively as a purgative. This is one of the last areas in South America to be populated by savage tribes who pound out messages on drums, kill missionaries, and shrink heads.

Virginia: Nancy, did you catch any of that?

Nancy: Not a word. Well, sarsaparilla, but that was it. *To Jack.* Thank you anyway.

He smiles and nods, then abruptly clutches at the side of his neck, grunts, and falls off the back of the boat.

Nancy: Oh dear!

Virginia: Nancy, what is it?

Nancy: It's our guide. I think he's been felled by a poison-tipped blow dart.

She looks over the edge at Jack, who confirms this with a nod, then slithers away.

Virginia: Oh no! Can we save him?

Nancy: I don't think so. He's too far downstream to reach now.

Virginia: But Nancy, this is terrible. We've no one to steer our frail craft and now it seems there are some sort of savages in the trees.

Nancy: We'd best hope that dart was meant to settle a personal matter. *Nancy cries out as though grazed by a dart. She sees another fly by at close range.*

Virginia: Nancy, what's happening?

Nancy: Better lie low Mrs. T. I'm going to paddle up a storm.

Virginia lies face down and stares ahead. Nancy paddles with ever increasing rapidity.

Nancy: There we go! Now we're picking up steam. I'm enjoying this a little and I'm sure I'll be healthier for it as well. Did you know I was on the women's sculling team at school? It wasn't quite like this of course . . . Oh no! I think we're headed for the rapids. Aieeeee!

Virginia: Nancy, wait a moment!

Nancy: Mrs. Tilford, I don't think we can.

Virginia: No, just consider for a moment, as we plunge headlong into this danger, that in only a few short hours, we'll be peacefully remembering these terrible moments as though they were nothing.

Nancy: I . . . oh . . . I see what you're saying.

They leap out of the boat and sit on the ground, where they recline and laugh.

Virginia: Oh Nancy, how brave you were today. How brave and fool-hardy and athletic!

Nancy: A gal's gotta be all those things if she's going to be shooting jungle rapids.

Virginia: I suppose you saved my life back there.

Nancy: Aw shucks. Twaren't nothin'.

Virginia: But it was something Nancy. I wonder how I can ever repay you.

Nancy: Mrs. Tilford, you pay me all the time.

Virginia: But this is different. I'm wondering if it maybe isn't time I invited you to address me by my given name.

Nancy: Oh, my goodness . . . Virginia . . .

Virginia: Yes, that's it. Say it again. Use my name in a sentence.

Nancy: It certainly is humid here, isn't it Virginia. Say Virginia, which bothers you more, small snakes or large insects?

Virginia: *Clasps Nancy's hands.* Oh Nancy, do you realize that no one has called me anything but Mrs. Tilford for ten years. Not since the day Weldon embraced me on the front doorstep and said. "Goodbye Virginia. I'll see you again in two months time." *She buries her face in her hands.*

Nancy: Oh Mrs. . . . Virginia . . . There there.

Virginia: I'm sorry, Nancy.

Nancy: No no, you cry all you want. Who's to notice here in the rain forest?

Virginia: I'm very tired Nancy, and it seems to be getting dark. I wonder if we ought to camp here for the night.

Nancy: I was just thinking that myself.

Virginia: I don't suppose I know how one camps. Do you?

Nancy: I think lying down must be a good start.

Virginia: Then let's do that.

They lie on their backs.

Virginia: It's so still. Only a few birds and insects break the silence.

From a corner of the room, Jack attempts a variety of bird and insect calls. Nancy tries a few surreptitiously as well.

Virginia: Nancy, what on earth are you doing?

Nancy: Oh . . . I . . . just trying to communicate with the wildlife.

Virginia: I didn't realize you had that skill.

Nancy: Oh yes. Wasn't a campfire girl for nothin' you know.

She gets to her knees and emits some squawks. Jack responds and they have a merry exchange.

Virginia: Nancy, I'm impressed that you can be such a chatterbox with our jungle friends, but I wonder if you haven't now got them a little excited.

Jack continues to make chirping sounds.

Virginia: Tell me, have we got the portable Victrola with us, or did we lose it in the rapids?

Nancy: No, it's right over there.

Virginia: Perhaps the sound of Rosa Ponselle might soothe the fauna and help us all to get a good night's rest.

Nancy: *Crossing to the phonograph* It's certainly worth a try.

She puts on a record and Ponselle's voice is heard singing from Verdi's Il Trovatore. Jack's bird-calls become more musical and gradually subside.

Virginia: Listen Nancy, I think the birds and the insects are in Rosa's thrall.

They sit quietly listening for a moment. Jack, now wearing a pith helmet slowly approaches and stands to one side.

Jack: Well well. Who've we got here?

Virginia: Oh!

Nancy: A man!

Virginia: Who are you sir? What do you want?

Nancy: Don't hurt us!

Jack: Please ladies, I've only come to satisfy my curiosity. It seemed there was a possibility that the great Rosa Ponselle was holding forth in this glade. Now I find it's only a phonographic representation, so instead I'll express my curiosity about who you might be and what you're doing here.

Nancy: We asked you first.

Jack: Of course you did. My name is Baxter Clark and I'm something of a botanist.

Virginia: Well that's a respectable calling in a locale of this sort. Mr. Clark, I'm Mrs. Virginia Tilford and this is Miss Nancy Kimble.

They shake hands warmly.

Virginia: I wonder which particular botanical avenue brings you here.

Jack: In a word Mrs. Tilford . . . drugs.

Virginia: Pardon me?

Jack: It's my belief that certain of the indigenous plant forms of South America have narcotic properties which could revolutionize modern medicine and improve the quality of life for many people all over the world.

Virginia: My goodness. Yours is a lofty pursuit.

Jack:	Yes yes, with some amusing angles as well. I have here some leaves which when nibbled provide one with sensations of an almost hallucinatory nature. Would you care to try them?
Nancy:	I think that I would.
Virginia:	We are in need of clarity and rest right now, as we are on a difficult quest.
Jack:	Oh? How's that?
Virginia:	We're in search of a silver mine, and more importantly some clues in the mysterious disappearance of my husband, Weldon Tilford of Providence, Rhode Island.
Jack:	Mmm. Can't say that dings a bell. And it's odd to think of there being a silver mine in the midst of this dense rain forest. Are you certain you're in the right—
Virginia:	Yes. I've a map which has led us right into this neck of the wet woods. *Opens up the map.* In fact, if I had a compass, I might verify—
Jack:	Mrs. Tilford, I have a compass right here.
Virginia:	Ah, bravo.
Jack:	And on comparison with your map, I see that you are . . . in exactly the place you want to be.
Virginia:	Really?
Jack:	Yes. Give or take a few yards.
Nancy:	So . . . should we dig?
Jack:	I think not here. The map puts the treasure over that way. Just in the lake, oddly enough.
Virginia:	The lake?

Jack: Yes, had you not noticed that there's a lake just over there?

Virginia: Well, it was already getting dark when we crawled up from the river over there.

Jack: But now the sun is coming up and you'll be able to see—

Virginia: The sun is rising? My word, but these equatorial nights are unpredictable in length. Excuse us, Mr. Clark, while we ensure that our faces are ready to bear the scrutiny of daylight.

Nancy: Oh dear, yes.

They turn their backs to him and take out compacts. They check their appearances in the little mirrors and dab and powder.

Jack: Good gracious! I see the most extraordinary thing.

Nancy: What is it Mr. Clark?

Jack: See there, above us and everywhere . . . there are glints of silver in the trees.

Nancy: *Flashes her compact mirror.* Yes, that would be from—

Jack: No! They're coming from the lake, I swear it.

Virginia: That's not so unusual. Water always sparkles in the sunlight.

Jack: Not like this, Mrs. Tilford. There is something extraordinary about this particular light. Something brilliant and . . . *Hurries upstage.* Look, there on the edge of the water. It's silver!

Nancy: Yes! Yes, it is. It looks like . . . a fork!

Jack: It is! And there's a spoon. And another larger one. A silver soup spoon!

Virginia: Is the lake full of silverware then?

Jack: I believe that it is. Here . . .

In the extreme upstage, he bends down and picks up a few items of silverware. He gives them to Nancy, the wipes his hands on his jacket.

Jack: Ladies, I've been a fool not to have realized the truth. Your map isn't the location of a mine at all. Rather, we have stumbled upon the legendary Silver lake of Orienté, and what we see scattered in its waters is the lost treasure of Eusebio de la Frappa.

Virginia: Please Mr. Clark, explain.

Jack: De la Frappa was one of the last conquistadors. He was vain and foolish and broke away from his countrymen, intending to build himself his own city in the midst of the rain forest. He and his followers carted all sorts of useless items along with them, including a collection of silverware that had been fashioned out of stolen Inca treasure. The men never reached their destination however and not long afterward, their shrunken heads were discovered strung up in the jungle. Nothing was ever found of their possessions, but rumours have persisted for years that the silverware was deposited in a lake for safe keeping and never claimed. Ladies, there it is!

Virginia: Well well, I'm stunned. That charlatan's map was entirely accurate. I wonder . . . Can Weldon have stood where now stand? Did he see this lake of silver?

Jack: *Peers off.* I think I see . . . Yes, just in a little deeper. There's a candelabra. Removes his shoes and socks. I'm going to wade in and get it. *He rolls his pant legs up a little and wades into a corner, where he picks up a candelabra.* Here you go, Nancy. That's for you. *He reaches over and she takes it from him.* And I think I may have spied a tea service just a little deeper in. I'll just look in and—

He wades back in as he says this, but suddenly gives a sharp cry and starts vibrating wildly.

Jack: YAAAAAARRR!!!

Nancy: Mr. Clark, what is it? What's happening?

Jack: It's ELECTRIC EELS!

Nancy: Oh no! you've got to get out of the water! Get out! Help!
I'll save you! *She runs to him and grabs his hand.*

Jack: NOOO!!!

*They stand together, screaming and vibrating, till she manages to pull
him abruptly back and he collapses on the ground. Nancy falls panting
on the ground beside him.*

Nancy: Mr. Clark! Mr. Clark, are you breathing?

She pounds on his chest and he coughs and sputters and sits up.

Jack: Oh my. I thought those slithery fiends had me in their
clutches for good.

Virginia: No Mr. Clark, thanks to Nancy's valour, you have survived.
You have survived what others surely have not. *She walks
away and stands with her back to them.*

Nancy: Mrs. Til . . . Virginia? Are you alright?

Virginia: Yes. Yes, I am. But now I know. My husband can only
have been a victim of these unwitting guardians of de la
Frappa's treasure.

Jack: I'm sorry Mrs. Tilford. It's a terrible thing to have disc—

Virginia: No Mr. Clark, I am glad of this knowledge. *Turning to
them.* If I might, I'd like to have a moment alone. Nancy,
I'd like you to fetch some things from our luggage if you
wouldn't mind.

*The two women go off and murmur together. Nancy exits. Jack takes his
shoes and socks and moves off to a distant corner, where he puts them on
while he watches as Virginia goes to the phonograph and puts on a
recording. It's Rosa Ponselle singing the "Ave Maria" from Verdi's* Otello.
She stands and listens intently for a few phrases until Nancy enters with

a basket containing a linen placemat, a plate, wine glass, and silverware. She hands these items to Virginia and withdraws to sit beside Jack. Virginia crosses to the place setting on the floor, kneels, and carefully places the silverware. She places the candelabra in front of the cloth, and lights the candles. Then she leans back and looks at what she's created.

Virginia: Here is your grave, Weldon Tilford. And on it finally, a monument in silver. For ten years I've kept a place setting for you at my table. Now there's one for you here, and that'll have to be sufficient.

She kisses her fingertips, then touches each element of the place setting lightly. She bows her head for a moment, then gets up and crosses and turns off the record. She turns and smiles at Jack and Nancy.

Virginia: My friends, I'm going to have to have a rest now.

Nancy: Of course Virginia. We have a long journey ahead, back up the river and—

Virginia: No. Nancy, Mr. Vail . . . I'm going upstairs to my bedroom.

Nancy: Oh . . . yes. Alright.

Virginia: Good afternoon, Mr. Vail.

Jack: Yes Mrs. Tilford, good afternoon.

She goes out. Nancy and Jack stand quietly for a moment, then look at one another.

Jack: Nancy, I'm going to go now too. She shouldn't . . . I don't think that—

Nancy: Yes Jack. Thank you.

He smiles and exits.

Scene Four
As Nancy extinguishes the candles, Jack stands in a separate light.

Jack: The week I spent in Providence following that afternoon was distinctly uneventful. It seemed to me that I had done the most significant thing I was ever destined to do in Rhode Island, and so I decided that I should be moving on come the following Monday. This meant I would be able to return to Saint Margaret's on Sunday, and I was eager to do this for two reasons. The first was because I had so enjoyed the service the previous week, and the second . . . Well, you can probably imagine what that was. The sermon was once again pleasantly inspirational and the singing was vehement and uplifting, but I saw no sign of Nancy or her employer. As before, we were invited to remain afterward for pie and conviviality and so I did, whereupon I received a most pleasant surprise. I spied the ladies across the parish hall, both eating pie and having an animated conversation.

Virginia and Nancy appear.

Jack: I was hesitant about approaching them, so I merely stood where I might be noticed. It was Mrs. Tilford who saw me first.

Virginia sees Jack and smiles. She murmurs to Nancy, who turns and gives a little wave. The women exchange a few more words and Virginia takes an envelope from her purse and gives to Nancy. Virginia takes Nancy's pie plate from her and exits as Nancy approaches Jack.

Nancy: Jack, I'm so pleased to see you.

Jack: Yes, I'm glad to see you too. I looked for you during the service, but—

Nancy: Oh, well we were sitting up near the front.

Jack: Ah, that's . . . Nancy, I think that's wonderful news.

Nancy: Jack, it is. *Hands Jack the envelope.* Virginia has asked me to give this to you.

Jack: Oh? *He opens the envelope and takes out a note and a cheque.* "Mr. Vail, in appreciation of your ability to see one through to the heart of the matter." Nancy, this is a lot of money.

Nancy: Oh, she can afford it. Especially now that she's selling her house.

Jack: Really? She's—

Nancy: Yes Jack. Virginia and I . . . We're going to travel.

Jack: You are? Anywhere in particular?

Nancy: No, I don't think so. Probably we'll go east and west before we head south, but basically we just want to see the world.

Jack: I think that's great. I'm leaving Providence as well.

Nancy: That doesn't surprise me. Have you a specific destination?

Jack: Not really. The world, same as you.

Nancy: Well good then Jack Vail. Maybe we'll see each other again.

Jack: Nancy Kimble, I know we will.

She smiles and exits.

Jack: I know we will. I can already imagine it.

Blackout

Cathy Derkach as Sheila, Jeff Haslam as Spence, Leona Brausen,
as Alice, and Ron Pederson as Leo in the Teatro La Quindicina
production of The Margin of the Sky, *Edmonton, Alberta, 2003.*

Photo: Kevin Wilson/SEE Magazine

The Margin of the Sky

Production History

The Margin of the Sky was first performed by Teatro La Quindicina at the Varscona Theatre in Edmonton in May, 2003.

CAST

Leo	*Ron Pederson*
Spence	*Jeff Haslam*
Alice	*Leona Brausen*
Sheila	*Cathy Derkach*

Director	*Stewart Lemoine*
Costume Designer	*Leona Brausen*
Set Designer	*Marissa Kochanski*
Lighting Designer	*Mike Takats*
Stage Manager	*Jana O'Connor*

Production Notes

CHARACTERS

Leo: a Canadian playwright in his mid-twenties
Spence: a soap opera star in his mid to late thirties
Alice: a bookkeeper in her early forties
Sheila: a dress shop owner in her late thirties

SETTING

Los Angeles, California, present day.

Marissa Kochanski's simple set for the Teatro premiere of *The Margin of the Sky* featured a wide and flexible playing space, framed by palm trees painted on a blue background which extended to the full height of the stage. The outdoor terrace was on a raised platform in the upper centre backed with a further expanse of blue. The patio furniture was present throughout, as were Leo's desk and computer, located at stage left. Other scenes were defined by minimal additions of furniture pieces which came and went as necessary. Mike Takats's lighting saturated most of the play with a great deal of warmth and colour, except for the three components of Scene Eleven which were somewhat starker.

NOTES

It should come as no surprise that musical selections are key in a play whose action is partly a consequence of the characters' reaction to Schoenberg's *Gurrelieder*. For the most part, the excerpts are from Sir Simon Rattle's recording with the Berlin Philharmonic on EMI, recorded with exceptional balance and fullness. The excerpts heard are as follows:

At the conclusion of Scene Three as Spence is left alone listening, the very beginning of the prelude is heard and this bridges the scene transition and fades as Alice and Leo begin speaking in Scene Four.

The music heard in the transition to Scene Five is the rapturous first statement of the main love theme which is heard immediately following Tove's "Den all meine rosen kusst ich zu Tod, dieweil ich deiner gedacht." The sound fades as Spence is observed listening during the scene proper, then fades in again at the expansive restatement of the same theme which occurs a few moments later, and this is played as a bridge to Scene Six.

The bridge to Scene Seven is Tove's final line, "ersterbend in seligen Kuss!" faded down during the high note on the last word.

In Scene Nine, the first music heard over the store speakers is the initial half-minute or so of the Orchestral Interlude following Waldemar's final line of Part One, "du wunderliche Tove." After stopping it abruptly, Leo resumes the Interlude just past two minutes into the piece, and the men shout their dialogue over what ensues. The ladies make their entrance about a minute later at around the three-minute mark, and the exact moment should be self-evident. Sheila's departure to turn down the music occurs about a minute later when the music has regained its volume.

The excerpts from "The Song of the Wood Dove" used for Scene Eleven are taken from Seiji Ozawa's recording of *Gurrelieder* with the Boston Symphony on the Phillips label. This is an absolute necessity, for what is important on this recording is the unmistakable voice of Tatiana Troyanos. As with the Rosa Ponselle recordings required in *Pith!*, there can be no substitution. Troyanos sings the

Wood Dove's music with a unique and arresting plangency of timbre, a sound which effectively lays bare the emotion beneath Leo's somewhat circumscribed responses to his disappointments. The first excerpt heard is simply the orchestral introduction which bridges the transition from Scene Ten, played up to the pause before the vocal entry about twenty seconds in. The second begins with the line, "Tod ist Tove," cued immediately following Leo's "But . . . Troyanos . . ." The final excerpt is cued by Leo after "I just don't want to talk about it right now. Not with you," and begins at the phrase "Weit flog ich, Klage sucht' ich und den Tod." Leo and Spence shout the final lines of their argument over this line, then Spence leaves Leo alone for "Helwig Falke war's der grausam Gurres Taube zerris!" and its aftermath as described in the script.

The final *Gurrelieder* excerpt heard is a return to the very opening of the Prelude, played underneath Leo's final paragraph and increasing in volume as he rejoins the group at the table and the scene light fades.

The music heard at the very top of the play is a recording of Brahms's "Gestillte Sehnsucht," sung by Marjana Lipovsek. It begins in darkness, with Leo observed writing and calculating during the viola solo introduction and the others being seen after the vocal entry. The excerpt heard at the end of the scene is "Gracia Mia" from *Canciones Amatorias* by Granados, as sung by Bernarda Fink.

For the transitions in and out of Sheila's dress shop, *Gurrelieder* is not so much on everyone's mind, and here some classic upbeat Dave Brubeck selections would be appropriate.

Prologue

The lights come up on Leo sitting at a desk looking at a small opened laptop computer. A mezzo-soprano is heard singing Brahms. Periodically, Leo types, but mostly he thinks. Another light comes up revealing Alice as she tastes a spoonful of chicken salad from a food processor bowl. As this establishes, another light illuminates Sheila opening a CD and looking at the packaging, then loading a portable player. Finally Spence appears, sitting with a script on the floor, looking at it, then not looking at it, committing lines to memory. As he does this he rolls onto his back and continues reading while slowly raising and lowering his knees as though riding a bicycle. Eventually, the light fades on all except Leo. He picks up a remote control and shuts off the music. He makes some notes on a piece of paper, then does some figures on a calculator.

Leo: Hmmm. Interesting.

He lifts the remote and cues another mezzo-soprano, this time singing something Spanish.

Fade

Scene One

Leo sits behind his desk. Spence straddles a chair beside him.

Leo: So he's walking along the street and he passes a nun and he says "Good morning sister," and she says "Good morning" and then we see her face and she's got a single tear rolling down her cheek, because you see, it is his sister. It's Maureen, and she's become a nun and now no one really sees her face and so you know they're just going to go on thinking she's dead even though she walks among them all the time.

Spence: Sort of like a ghost?

Leo: Right. But worse in a way.

Spence: It's worse to be alive?

Leo: Well I'd think so. If you're having to live like a ghost you should at least be dead.

Spence: Okay, maybe I follow that. And being dead would have other advantages.

Leo: It would?

Spence: Wouldn't it? I'm asking you.

Leo: You know, I don't think the fine points of this are what really matter. The thing is the irony of the final exchange. He calls her sister and she is his sister.

Spence: And she cries.

Leo: Credits roll.

Spence: It's a sad ending.

Leo: It's a sad story.

Spence: So maybe the end should be more—

Leo: What, happy? It's not totally unhappy. It's not devastating if you think about it. She's still got her ironic perspective. Right now it's making her cry, but that just shows how alive she is. If she can see the irony in a sad situation, that means she's got a good chance of finding her sense of humour at some point in the future. Maybe that very afternoon. And life at the convent is probably A-okay. She's got a roof over her head. She gets her three square a day. Unless she's a Carmelite in which case she fasts a lot and lies face down on the floor.

Spence: We could pad her habit a bit, so people will see that she's a nun who eats.

Leo: We could.

Spence: But they might think she's pregnant.

Leo:	They won't. They aren't going to have time to even look. This is a few seconds. It's a long shot of her approaching, then a medium shot from behind her as they pass. Then the close-up of her face.
Spence:	With the tear?
Leo:	That's right.
Spence:	Sad. She's like a ghost. Only worse.
Leo:	Don't dwell on that. She's like a ghost. And she's alright with that.
Spence:	She could laugh.
Leo:	Instead of crying?
Spence:	It's happier.
Leo:	"Good morning sister." "Good morning." Close-up. It's Maureen. She laughs.
Spence:	Credits roll. We could shoot it both ways.
Leo:	Yeah, we could.
Spence:	You don't like my idea.
Leo:	No no, I . . . Well yes. I don't like it. But my idea is the big one here. And you don't like it. And I don't mean the big big idea, because that was yours.
Spence:	And do you still like it?
Leo:	Sure I do. But it's an idea. It's not so tangible that you can lavish a lot of liking on it. Choices need to be made. Clarifications.
Spence:	Well Leo, maybe you should write it. You should just write the screenplay.

Leo: Well I guess I walked into that one. You know Spence, I think I'm going to. A lot will fall into place when I write it. That's how it goes. Things settle. They change. *Pause.* Do you still actually want to do this?

Spence: What, this idea?

Leo: This whole project. You're not conflicted, now that you and Carol are—

Spence: No, not at all. This is separate. My problems are with her, not you. And they're not even problems. It's just over.

Leo: Divorce is good for people.

Spence: That's how I see it.

Leo: So you're enjoying it? What if it's addictive, like going to the chiropractor?

Spence: It's certainly less pleasant than that. Divorce is a positive step, that's all I was trying to say.

Leo: So do you still go to the chiropractor?

Spence: No. I think I'm done with that too, thanks to Pilates.

Leo: Oh yeah? You're giving that a whirl?

Spence: Sure. A lot of the cast are doing it. I'm just a beginner but I did buy a mat. Claire's been breaking me in slowly.

Leo: Claire?

Spence: From the show. She plays Maeve. *Pause.* Corinne's sister. The nurse.

Leo: Of course.

Spence: You haven't been watching in a while.

Leo: Is that a problem?

Spence:	No, whatever. I don't care. Daytime drama isn't for everyone. But you should see Claire. She's interesting.
Leo:	She's the nurse?
Spence:	She's the actress who plays the nurse.
Leo:	Right. She's breaking you in.
Spence:	I think she's talented. She's got a nice . . . quality. She's . . .
Leo:	She should be in our movie?
Spence:	I think you'd like her. She might be our Maureen.
Leo:	Okay now I'm a little uncomfortable.
Spence:	What? Why?
Leo:	A few reasons I suppose. This woman, your trainer—
Spence:	Claire?
Leo:	She's just a friend?
Spence:	Yeah. Well no. Things could happen . . . that haven't yet.
Leo:	Because you're still married to my sister.
Spence:	I thought you didn't have a conflict with that.
Leo:	I didn't. But I may now. A conflict that would be your fault.
Spence:	The divorce'll be final in a few weeks. At the rate we've been going, you're not going to be in any conflict because you still won't have started writing.
Leo:	Maybe not, but I'll have had to be having to think about all this. The thinking is important. The thinking and thinking and thinking . . . Plus I have to be able to look Carol in the face and not have to conceal the fact that while I'm

being supportive and comforting to her in this difficult time, I'm also creating a magnificent starring vehicle for her successor.

Spence: Her successor? Carol's a makeup artist. She was never even—

Leo: I'm aware of that. Maybe you need to consider this though . . . Jack is Maureen's brother. It's an intimate sibling relationship and I don't think it's appropriate that you undertake something of that nature with your new girlfriend.

Spence: That's not what she is.

Leo: Yet.

Spence: Well it had occurred to me that maybe Jack and Maureen don't have to be related.

Leo: But you're the one who insisted . . . No romance! No more heartthrob crap!

Spence: That doesn't mean Maureen can't just be a girl from the neighbourhood that Jack simply cares for a great deal.

Leo: Because she helped him with his flexibility.

Spence: Don't make fun. Claire's a good actress. She trained . . . probably.

Leo: Okay look, here's the thing. If she's not your sister then there's no point to the nun thing. You remember . . . "Good morning sister." And she is his his sister. Irony. Curtain.

Spence: Well maybe she doesn't have to be a nun.

Leo: If she's not a nun, he'd probably recognize her.

Spence: She could be wearing a what's that . . . that Muslim thing . . .

Leo:	A bourka?
Spence:	Yeah! They cover up even more than those nun hats.
Leo:	Why would she . . . Oh, never mind. She's not going to wear a bourka. People see women in those and they think they aren't supposed to talk to them at all.
Spence:	But it's not really true. People should probably be enlightened about that.
Leo:	So he says what? "Good morning Sheherezade."
Spence:	Just "Good morning" is probably fine. And she says "Good morning" back, or nods . . .
Leo:	And where is the irony in all this?
Spence:	Well . . . He thinks he doesn't know her . . . but really he does.

Leo abruptly slides out of his chair and lies on the floor behind his desk.

Spence:	You don't like my idea.
Leo:	Maybe I don't. Let's table the discussion for a bit. I need to write the script. I need to start.
Spence:	Yeah. That's probably a good first step. And I should go. I have to learn lines and then I have an appointment.
Leo:	For some bendies?
Spence:	Not quite. I'm seeing my chiropractor.
Leo:	I thought you gave that up.
Spence:	I have. I just need to end it formally.
Leo:	Isn't that what not making an appointment is for?
Spence:	You just wait. You'll have health and fitness issues one day

and you'll experience the intricate emotional network they involve.

Leo: I got no respect. Not for nobody.

Spence: That's not true. You're a good and devoted brother and a loyal friend and colleague.

Leo: Uh-huh, thanks. *Gets up from the floor.* Oh. You're being sincerely complimentary.

Spence: Yeah, I guess I am. You're great. You just need to work a lot harder than you do.

Leo: Okay. I'll start. After lunch probably.

Spence: Or whenever.

Leo: No, I'll do it. The midday meal is key. Sustenance followed by renewal. That's the glory of lunch and I've been neglecting its possibilities. Tell ya what . . . You come back at four and I'll have five pages of actual dialogue you can look at. Guaranteed.

Spence: Well that'd be great, but three-thirty is when my appointment is scheduled and they're always way behind and then I'd have to drive all the way back here from Santa Monica— . . .

Leo: Okay fine, you don't want to, but I might fail without the incentive.

Spence: Well then you come to me. Meet me at the chiropractor's with something good at about four-thirty, quarter to five and I'll take you for coffee and we can discuss it.

Leo: Coffee? In Santa Monica at five o'clock?

Spence: Okay fine, margaritas.

Leo: *Rolls his eyes.* Kuh.

Spence:	*Takes a card from his wallet.* This is the address. I'm off now. Have a good lunch, and if you eat for five bucks instead of ten, you probably won't need a nap by two.
Leo:	Is that a tip from Claire?
Spence:	I think it was Denise.
Leo:	Did I meet her? Who did she play?
Spence:	She wasn't on the show. *Pause.* We actually aren't going to talk about her ever.
Leo:	Oh. I get it. Bastard.
Spence:	Uh-huh. See ya Leo.
Leo:	See ya.

Spence exits.

Leo:	Ten bucks . . . Who's got that?

Blackout.

Scene Two

Alice is sitting on a park bench eating a sandwich. Leo passes carrying a nearly empty bottle of water. He feels something in his shoe and stops to examine it. As he does this, Alice begins choking. She tries to clear her throat and becomes increasingly desperate, flailing her arms to get Leo's attention. He's initially put out by her frantic gesticulation, but eventually she conveys her plight.

Leo:	Oh. Oh dear. Oh heaven. Oh no!

He hurries to her and grabs her from behind and squeezes her in various creative ways until she gasps, coughs and is able to breathe again.

Leo:	There. I think we got it. How are you feeling? What happened?

Alice:	A bone. There must have been a bone.
Leo:	In your sandwich?
Alice:	It was chicken salad. That can sometimes happen.
Leo:	But you're all clear now? It's out?
Alice:	Yes, it seems to be.
Leo:	I guess there's no halfway with choking.
Alice:	That's right. You're either doing it or you just aren't. *Pause.* Thanks for the assistance.
Leo:	Oh, sure. Glad to help. Should we look for the bone?
Alice:	Why?
Leo:	Well you could take it back to wherever you got your sandwich. You could get a refund. Maybe exchange it for something else. Egg salad. No. There might be shells in that.
Alice:	Actually, I made the sandwich myself. I brought it from home.
Leo:	What? You made your own chicken salad? People do that?
Alice:	It's easy with a food processor.
Leo:	Do you make your own mayo?
Alice:	No, I'm not that industrious. I use Hellman's.
Leo:	So that, and chicken, and . . .
Alice:	A little salt and pepper. Sometimes some chopped onion. Green onion.
Leo:	Scallions?
Alice:	There you are. Celery. Sometimes. And a little garlic salt. A little.

Leo:	Sounds just great.

Alice: It is. I don't think I can finish this now though. I'm a little spooked.

Leo: I bet it's okay. You could just chew carefully.

Alice: That's good advice in general I think. *She lifts the sandwich and peers at it.* No. No, I really don't want it right now.

Leo: Throw it away then. I wouldn't judge you for it. I wouldn't think you were wasteful.

Alice: Mayo doesn't really keep. Do you want it? I haven't even taken a bite of the other half.

Leo: Oh, no, I— . . . No thank you.

Alice: Yes, I'm sorry. What am I thinking? I was just choking on this.

Leo: Actually, you know, I'm a little curious. I'll bet it's delicious. Homemade chicken salad . . . and Hellman's. What's irresistible if not that? I'll have a bite.

Alice: Would you? I'd find that comforting. Please be careful.

Leo: I'll taste it . . . gingerly.

Alice: A little ginger might be nice in a chicken salad. And some raisins . . .

He takes the sandwich and takes a small bite. He chews very meticulously, mostly with his front teeth.

Leo: Oh, that's very nice. I feel privileged to have enjoyed this and regret that it had to happen under these circumstances.

Alice: Oh well. A happy outcome after a nasty event. You were helpful and you get a reward.

Leo:	Everybody wins. I get a sandwich and you get to live.
Alice:	Oh . . . *She stares ahead. Her mouth is slightly open.*
Leo:	What's wrong?
Alice:	I could have died. I would have. I've often eaten lunch alone here. If I'd been alone today . . .
Leo:	You'd better not think about that.
Alice:	I can't help it. I'm going to think about it all day. Every time I see something or talk to someone . . . I'm going to be thinking "Well this wouldn't be happening. This wouldn't have happened." On the bus I'll think "This seat would have been empty." I'm going to get home and think "Well this would be about when they call my parents and my brothers to tell them," and in a couple of days I'll wake up and think "I'd have been buried today probably." I don't know that my life will ever be normal again.
Leo:	But on the whole you're pleased?
Alice:	I should be. I should. I'm Alice. What's your name?
Leo:	Leo.

She bursts into tears.

Leo:	Oh my.
Alice:	Leo saved my life!
Leo:	I didn't. I didn't. Okay, I did.
Alice:	*Sobbing.* I'm so sorry. I'm sorry for crying.
Leo:	It's fine. You're doing it because you're happy. Which is ironic and therefore makes me happy in a whole other unrelated way.
Alice:	What?

Leo:	Never mind. Nothing.
Alice:	*Still sobbing.* You can go if you want to.
Leo:	I don't know . . . You maybe don't want to be alone when you're all emotional like this. Or . . . actually . . . *Squints pensively.* I think I would want to be alone. If I was emotional. But in such times as these, do we really know what's best for us?
Alice:	I'm sure I'll be better in a few minutes.
Leo:	Do you want me to call someone for you?
Alice:	No, you don't have to. It should pass. It should—
Leo:	You're right, it should. But Alice, don't try to make it unimportant.

She looks at him, then takes his hand and squeezes it.

Alice:	You saved my life Leo!

She cries some more. He gives her a little hug. She hugs back with greater intensity.

Leo:	Oh . . . Watch . . . Oop . . .
Alice:	What? Oh . . . sorry sorry sorry . . . I shouldn't—
Leo:	No, it's just. The sandwich was pushing against my—
Alice:	Oh! Oh no! Mayonnaise is hard to get out of—
Leo:	But it didn't . . . Here. *Puts it aside.* You've caused enough trouble there Mr. Chick-Sal-Sammy.
Alice:	You're sure there's no stain?
Leo:	There really isn't. Alice, may I make a suggestion?
Alice:	Sure.

Leo:	*Stands.* Let's get up and move away from here. I feel a strange kind of lingering bad energy and I don't ever talk or think that way so I've gotta take it seriously. You probably need a drink.
Alice:	Oh—
Leo:	I mean a beverage. A liquid.
Alice:	*Stands.* I think you're right. You're coming with me?
Leo:	I am. Your body's had a shock. I think it needs fluids and companionship. I can provide those things.
Alice:	What a good citizen you are!
Leo:	Why thank you, I appreciate that. Amusingly, I'm actually a Canadian involved in a kind of a questionable employment set-up, so for you to say that is—
Alice:	It's ironic?
Leo:	Exactly. Like crying for joy. Like laughing at death.

She bursts into tears.

Leo:	Oh God, I'm sorry.
Alice:	No, I'm fine. I really am.

They exit.

Scene Three

In the chiropractor's office waiting room. Spence and Sheila are in chairs. She has earphones and a portable CD player and is following the liner notes. He's reading a magazine. Periodically they look up, occasionally meeting one another's glance and then looking away. After a while she removes her headphones.

Sheila:	Can you hear this? Is it bothering you?

Spence:	No. I can't hear anything at all.
Sheila:	Okay, good. I just never can quite accept that. It's fairly intense music.
Spence:	What, some kind of thrash thing?
Sheila:	No. Schoenberg.
Spence:	Oh.
Sheila:	Not extra-cranky Schoenberg. Just— . . . You know . . . I think we may have met before.
Spence:	Really?
Sheila:	Somewhere. Somehow. You just seem familiar . . . in a way.
Spence:	Actually, I think I probably know why. I'm . . . I'm on TV.
Sheila:	Oh yeah?
Spence:	In the afternoon. Weekday afternoons.
Sheila:	*Gasps.* Ohhh! I remember! You washed my car!
Spence:	What?
Sheila:	Yeah. You don't remember? A little green '96 Tercel.
Spence:	What?
Sheila:	It was at that celebrity charity fundraisy thing.
Spence:	Oh! *Covers his face with his hands.* Ohhhh!
Sheila:	Yeah, that's where it was. I remember your remarkable . . . short shorts.
Spence:	Those were supplied.

Sheila: Oh, take a little credit.

Spence: Yeah, okay, thanks.

They laugh uncomfortably, but not unhappily.

Spence: So did I do a good job? Was your car clean?

Sheila: I think so. I didn't really check. It may not have been dirty.

Spence: Well I'm . . . I'm . . . very embarrassed.

Sheila: Please, no, that's not necessary.

Spence: I guess you're right.

Pause.

Sheila: My name's Sheila.

Spence: I'm Spence.

Sheila: I'm pleased to meet you Spence. Formally.

Spence: Likewise. So Sheila, what is it you're listening to?

Sheila: Oh this? "Gurrelieder."

Spence: Girl Eater?

Sheila: Gurre Lieder. Songs of Gurre. Which is a place.

Spence: It's intense . . . you said?

Sheila: Yeah, but beautiful too. Loudly beautiful. Some of the intensity is also of a verbal kind. *Reads.* "The scudding clouds have gathered close against the margin of the sky."

Spence: Is that a good thing?

Sheila: It's part of a beautiful experience.

Spence: For the clouds?

Sheila: For the observers. The cloud activity is a sign of the approaching twilight, and that excites a pair of lovers who can only meet at night.

Spence: I don't think I remember what scudding means.

Sheila: To move along in a hurry. Scudding clouds would be driven by the wind.

Spence: That doesn't sound beautiful. Sounds dramatic.

Sheila: No, but the thing is that they've gathered by the margin of the sky.

Spence: So their scudding is done?

Sheila: That's right. "The limpid sea-waves all have lulled themselves to rest."

Spence: Calm waters.

Sheila: Very calm. "Westward, the sun throws off her purple robes and dreams upon her couch among the waves, of all the glory of the coming day."

Spence: Uhhh . . . I think I get that.

Sheila: It's all pretty exhausting, even as a beautiful experience.

Spence: I was gonna say.

Sheila: What are you reading?

Spence: SWF, 34, seeks SWM, 28-38. Enjoys cycling, camping, swimming, tennis, jazz concerts, travel, home renovations, automotive repair, and the study of languages. No head games.

Sheila: That also seems exhausting.

Spence: Doesn't it. I don't think I'm going to call her. *Pause.* I'm not actually looking for a date. I don't know why I'm reading this.

Sheila: I think there's an *Atlantic Monthly* sitting there.

Spence: Yeah, I saw it. It's just . . . not the current issue.

Sheila: Of course it isn't. *Pause.* Well . . . back to beauty. *She starts to put her headphones back in.*

Spence: *Quickly.* So what is it exactly? An opera?

Sheila: Not quite. It's an epic poem set to music. It's translated from the Danish. To the German. The English is here too though.

Spence: So someone's singing?

Sheila: Usually. Not all the time. People sing what they think and then the orchestra backs them up or contradicts them or lets you know what's happening weather-wise . . .

Spence: That sounds incredible. I didn't know this kind of thing went on.

Sheila: Do you want to listen to a bit?

Spence: Uh . . . sure.

Sheila: Well . . . here . . . *Hands him the headphones.* I'll just cue it here and . . .

He puts the headphones on, listens intently for a while, then takes them off.

Spence: That's fantastic.

Sheila: Isn't it.

Spence: What a rich experience to have in a waiting room. It's just so . . . smart of you. My brother-in-law listens to things like this. Quite a lot. Probably too much. It keeps him from working.

Sheila: Your brother-in-law? Your sister's husband?

Spence: Uh, no. He's the brother of . . . His sister is my wife. Was my wife.

Sheila: Aha. You were wearing a wedding band when you washed my car.

Spence: You remember that?

Sheila: Well yeah. It was one of two things you had on.

Spence: You know, I got a new agent after that event.

Sheila: And he said ditch the ring?

Spence: No, that was a whole different negotiation.

Sheila: Ah. Well it was prudent of you to wear it that day . . . so people wouldn't get the wrong idea. Or the other wrong idea.

There is a pause.

Sheila: So . . . chronic back pain? Or just trying to get a little extra height for an awards show, orrrr . . . ?

Spence: *Laughs.* Neither. I'm just here to . . . I'm here to tell the doctor I won't be coming in anymore. I had a little alignment issue, but I've found a more effective treatment. And it's cheaper.

Sheila: Well tell all, for God's sake.

Spence: It's just beginner Pilates.

Sheila: Get outta town.

Spence: It's pretty simple. It's like it looks on TV.

Sheila: You go to a class?

Spence: No, I study privately. The basics are . . . pretty basic.

Sheila: Could you show me?

Spence: Now? Here? I don't know about that. Oh, she's waving for you. The nurse.

Sheila: I believe she's just a receptionist.

Spence: Yeah, you're probably right. They trick you with those uniforms.

Sheila: It's all kind of dubious, isn't it. We're smart if we kick this. I can't back out now though. I'd have to pay anyway. Will you still be here when I'm done?

Spence: I expect so. I'm the next patient.

Sheila: Right. *Pause.* I'm just going to leave these CDs and my player with you.

Spence: Oh. Okay.

Sheila: I could put them in my bag and take them in with me, but then there'd be no particular reason for us to talk when I come out.

Spence laughs.

Spence: Also I can listen to a little more of this.

Sheila: That too. *Calls off.* Okay, I'm coming! *Muttering.* Ya registered nitwit. *To Spence.* Don't forget the booklet there. It's got the words.

Spence: *Picks it up.* Oh right. There's a booklet. This is just fantastic.

He resumes listening. The opening of "Gurrelieder" is heard as the lights fade.

Scene Four

Leo and Alice are sitting on grass and sipping from large Styrofoam cups.

Alice: This is fantastic. It's great. Who knew about smoothies!

Leo: I'm surprised you wouldn't actually.

Alice: Why's that?

Leo: Well since you make your own chicken salad. Chopping, blending, puréeing . . . It's all a similar kind of fun, I'd think.

Alice: That does make sense. I don't own a blender though. And liquids are a mistake in the food processor.

Leo: Yeah?

Alice: They splash out.

Leo: Because of the above average centrifugal force relative to the height of the unit and the lack of a watertight seal?

Alice: Yes.

Leo: You should get a blender.

Alice: I know. I love fruit. I just never thought to do this to it.

Leo: And you can add things. Extra fibre's what I always ask for. To me that feels like you're getting a little boost of character. It's really just oat bran, but you spin it however you need to.

Alice: Is oat bran still miraculous? Doesn't it just completely flush out your cholesterol?

Leo: I think it used to. What flavour did you get?

Alice: It's a Peach Tsunami. With extra calcium. Good for the bones.

Leo: Right. *He looks at her.*

Alice: What? Oh . . . I mentioned bones.

Leo: Yeah.

Alice: You thought I was gonna blow? Well, no. I think maybe I'm past the silly phase.

Leo: I don't think it was silly. To cry like that . . .

Alice: Well I didn't mean silly exactly . . . No, I did. I meant silly, but I didn't mean it in a critical way.

Leo: Yeah, I get ya. More like the putty than the goose?

Alice: There ya go.

Leo: Emotionally elastic . . . stretchy . . . kind of fun . . .

Alice: It even bounces.

Leo: I'd stay in that phase all day. Don't you have to go back to work?

Alice: No, not really. I kind of make my own hours. I'm a bookkeeper for a few small businesses. I work in one place in the morning and usually a different one in the afternoon. And not always the same ones.

Leo: So you're not expected anywhere?

Alice: That's right. If I don't come in, no one really thinks anything of it.

They sit gravely for a moment.

Leo: Well we should let that go. So bookkeeping . . . Is that hard? Fun? Nerve-racking?

Alice: It's pretty painless for me.

Leo: Because it isn't your money?

Alice:	Because I'm good at adding and subtracting. I used to be an actress though.
Leo:	Really? But you stopped.
Alice:	I guess I did. It wasn't a really active choice. I didn't get a lot of parts. Then I got even less. And I got more book-keeping jobs.
Leo:	But that shouldn't mean you're not an actress anymore.
Alice:	Well I don't act.
Leo:	I'm a writer and I mostly just talk and think.
Alice:	But that's probably a choice you're making.
Leo:	Yeah, okay, whatever. Stop picking on me. Where did you act?
Alice:	I was in plays. A couple in Los Angeles and more in . . . in the Pacific Northwest. And I was on TV a few times. I was on *Knot's Landing*.
Leo:	Oh, say.
Alice:	I sold Donna Mills a coat.
Leo:	Really? You rang in her purchase?
Alice:	I think her character had an account. I put it in the garment bag and handed it to her.
Leo:	Was she appreciative?
Alice:	She said thanks. It was in the script. So what do you write? Or what are you not writing?
Leo:	Oh . . . a . . . a screenplay for a movie. It's for my brother-in-law to be in. He's a soap star. Spence Collier from *The Lives We Borrow*.

She shrugs.

Leo: It's okay. I don't watch either. Anyway, Spence wants to produce this movie independently. So it's small. A small movie. A indie. With a non-existent script. I have it all worked out though, except when I change my mind about everything.

Alice: Have you written a script before?

Leo: I wrote some plays. Short ones. Medium-sized ones.

Alice: And you were pleased with them?

Leo: Oh yeah. People liked them. Canadian people.

Alice: Right, you're Canadian. You said that. You're working illegally.

Leo: Well technically I'm sort of "not working" illegally.

Alice: Are you having a problem?

Leo: I don't think so. I've only been here a couple of months. It's important to settle in. Spence . . . my brother-in-law . . . has me set up in a little office. He pays for it and that seems generous but he really does need the tax write-off.

Alice: So he's . . .

Leo: He married my sister. Carol. She convinced him to give me a break. I think she nagged a bit. Now they're getting a divorce.

Alice: Oh, so you're caught in the middle?

Leo: I am. It's kind of exciting. My home was very stable.

Alice: Mine was too.

Leo: You're not married?

Alice: No. Not for want of being asked though.

Leo: Asked a lot?

Alice: Well yeah, but just by the one guy . . . who'd have been a
          widower today.

Leo: Do you want to seek him out and give him another
          chance?

Alice: Not even a little. Which is new and a bit thrilling. I don't
          even want to think about him. Tell me about what you do.
          You wrote little plays for Canadians, and now you're writ-
          ing a movie. What's it going to be about?

Leo: It's hard to describe. Crime. A criminal. Spence's out to
          shake up his image.

Alice: Is it funny?

Leo: No, not particularly. That's kinda not his thing. Which is
          too bad.

Alice: I'd have expected you'd want to write a funny movie.

Leo: I guess I do. I forget to think about what I want some-
          times.

Alice: So have you been kind of blocked and miserable?

Leo: Not really. More . . . distracted. There always seem to be
          more pressing matters that need my attention.

Alice: Such as?

Leo: Well . . . there's a lot of smog here, so handwashing sweaters
          is more of a priority than it used to be, and then . . . there
          are a lot of lists that need to be made.

Alice: Such as . . . ?

Leo: Well, for example, someone has to rank the world's cur-
          rent top ten mezzo-sopranos. And that means comparing

recordings and making notes and then tabulating with a four-point system, which is the fairest method of making an objective decision based on subjective conclusions, but it is exhausting.

Alice: I'll bet it is. So who's leading the pack?

Leo: This week it's Marjana Lipovsek. Last week was Bernarda Fink. They're both Slovenian, interestingly enough, though the latter was born in Argentina. She's Argentine-Slovenian. There's no shorter way to say that.

Alice: Leo, you're just a marvellous person.

Leo: Thank you Alice.

Alice: You'll never marry.

Leo: I'm accepting of that.

Alice: Good. *Pause. She looks at her smoothie.* You know what'd be great in these?

Leo: What?

Alice: Rum.

Leo: You're completely right.

Alice: Let's go make that happen right now. Or do you need to get back to work?

Leo: Are you making fun of me?

Alice: No. I think you'd hate that.

Leo: I'm supposed to have five pages written by four-thirty.

They start to go.

Alice: That's hours away. How much time do you need?

Leo: Not that much. Maybe you can even help.

Alice:	I don't know how I'd do that.
Leo:	You'll keep me from being funny by being a constant reminder of lurking mortality.
Alice:	Or I could wash your sweaters.
Leo:	That'd work too. Let's go get rummy.

They exit.

Scene Five

At the chiropractor's office Spence is still listening with headphones. As the scene begins the music he's hearing plays out loudly, but fades as the lights come up, so he's the only one who can hear. He sits and listens intently, following his little booklet, reacting minimally, until something obviously strikes him. He drops the booklet and sits up very straight and listens with his eyes open wide for a moment, then slips on a pair of sunglasses. The music he's hearing swells up as the lights fade.

Scene Six

Leo is at his desk and Alice sits beside him. They're still sipping from their big cups.

Leo:	So finally, when the smoke has cleared and everyone's mostly gone to jail, we see Jack walking alone down a street and he passes a nun and he says "Good morning sister," and she says "Good morning" and then . . . we see her face and she's got a single tear rolling down her cheek, because . . . it is his sister.
Alice:	Get outta here!
Leo:	It is. It's Maureen, and she knows she can't ever show her face again after what happened, so she's become a nun and now no one really sees her face and so you know they're just going to go on thinking she's dead even though she isn't and she's right there.

Alice:	And she cries and they walk on in opposite directions.
Leo:	Exactly. Credits roll.
Alice:	Leo, that's just beautiful.
Leo:	Thank you.
Alice:	I love it. It's just like *Sea Wife*.
Leo:	What?
Alice:	You don't know it? I would have thought—
Leo:	No! NO!!
Alice:	Joan Collins and Richard Burton . . . She's a nun and he's a soldier and they're marooned on a tropical island and they almost have an affair and then they get rescued and much later she passes him on the street in her habit—
Leo:	And he doesn't recognize her.
Alice:	*With a gentle British inflection.* "No one ever looks at the face of a nun."
Leo:	Well crap. Crap! *He sits.* At least the idea seems based on a sound principle.
Alice:	*Sits.* Your use of it may be even more effective. And the other ninety-nine per cent of your movie is totally different.
Leo:	But that was my favourite part! I don't like the rest of it! I don't like the rest of it at all! What did you say that title was?
Alice:	*Sea Wife*.
Leo:	What the hell? Not Sea Sister? And Joan Collins was a nun? I object to this movie!
Alice:	I'm sorry I mentioned it.

Leo: No, I'm glad you did. Now we can start with a clean slate. A blank page.

Alice: Well technically—

Leo: Yeah, yeah, I know. They were all blank anyway, but there's just a better feeling in the air. You Alice, have saved me from a huge potential embarrassment.

Alice: And just think. *Ominously.* That almost didn't happen.

Leo: *Squeezes her hands.* Ohhhh. Yeeeeaaaahhhh . . .

Alice: Do we have more rum?

He holds up two little bottles, which are empty.

Leo: Sorry.

Alice: That's alright. Maybe it's time for work.

Leo: Maybe. But I don't know where to begin now. I can't imagine getting five whole pages done by— *Looks at his watch.* Oh-oh. That's crummy. I have to go. Do you want to come to Santa Monica?

Alice: Well yeah.

Leo: Good. You can meet my famous brother-in-law. He might be mad at me, but if you're there he'll have to pretend he isn't. That'll be funny and also . . . margaritas.

Alice: Whoo-hoo.

Leo: And we get to take the bus!

Alice: Yay!

They exit quickly.

Scene Seven

At the chiropractor's office, Spence is sitting as before, very intently listening with headphones to Sheila's disc player. He's following along in the little booklet and doesn't notice when Sheila returns and approaches him.

Sheila: *Waves a little.* Hello. Hello. HEY!

Spence sits up startled and takes out the headphones and removes his glasses.

Spence: Oh, sorry. You're done. That was fast.

Sheila: Was it?

Spence: I don't know. I've just been listening to this and I . . . *Looks at his watch.* I don't know what . . . uhhhh . . .

Sheila: Is something wrong?

Spence: This is a pretty awe-inspiring piece of music.

Sheila: You think so?

Spence: I've never heard anything like this. The singers are so loud. And they just suddenly aren't. And it's so happy and I already know it's going to be so sad later and awful and— . . . I . . . uhhh . . .

Sheila: Are you a bit of a mess over it?

Spence: No. It's totally good.

Sheila: Were you crying?

Spence: No.

Sheila: Your eyes are shiny.

Spence: I think they always are.

Sheila: Wow. Kudos.

Spence: *Holds up the player.* I guess you want this back.

Sheila: Sure, in a bit. Spence, you have to tell me what's so great. Is there something specific?

He looks at her, then looks away. He opens the book and finds a line.

Spence: "I have kissed my roses unto death, the while I thought of you."

Sheila looks at him for a moment, then at the booklet, then back at him.

Sheila: Oh my.

Spence: I gotta get outta here.

Sheila: But you still have to see the doctor.

Spence: Not really. They can bill me. They have my card on file. Come on. Come with me.

Sheila: Sure, but what do you want to do?

Spence: I don't know.

Sheila: Do you need to hear the rest of this?

Spence: I do. Not now though. I just need a little air. Or do you want it back?

Sheila: You better keep it handy.

Spence: Alright, good, thanks. How was your session?

Sheila: Fine actually. A real picker-upper. Huzzah! *Tosses her head.* Ow! *Clutching her neck.* Shouldn'a done that.

They exit quickly.

Scene Eight

Leo and Alice are walking briskly. Leo is looking at the card with the address.

Leo: I guess it's probably that building right there. *Looks at his watch.* And it's just four-thirty. We may actually be a little early.

Alice: Are you going to go up? Should I wait for you here?

Leo: No, of course not. You're supposed to meet Spence. You have to be there so he'll be nice to me.

Alice: I might be nervous.

Leo: Play it up. I think he likes that. Not too twitchy though.

Alice: Can I just nod and smile?

Leo: Yeah, but it'd be better if— . . . Aw hell, what am I thinking, telling you what to do. It's your day Alice. Do you want to come up?

Alice: Of course I do.

Leo: Well then let's— *Looks off.* What the— . . . That's him. Spence! Hey!! Spence!! Don't walk away!

Alice: Oh my God! He's that guy?

Leo: It's Leo! *Points at himself.* Uh-huh! Uh-huh! *To Alice.* There we go. He's coming. You alright?

Alice: I don't think so.

Leo: Who's the skirt I wonder?

Spence and Sheila enter.

Spence: Hi. You're here!

Leo: Yeah, I'm not late am I?

Spence:	I guess you're not.
Leo:	But you are leaving?
Spence:	Yeah, I'm . . . a little ahead of schedule.
Leo:	You weren't going to wait for me?
Spence:	I . . . Leo, I forgot you were coming.
Leo:	I see.
Spence:	We just decided that all so quickly and— . . . I'm going to have to look at your stuff some other time. I'm sorry. You wanted to go for drinks and—
Leo:	Don't sweat it, it's fine. I'm actually here to tell you I didn't get anything done.
Spence:	You came all this way to tell me that?
Leo:	Well I wasn't going to just not show and leave you sitting in the waiting room. Waiting and waiting . . . for nothing.
Spence:	Which is what you brought.
Leo:	Yes yes, the irony is palpable, just like in fiction. And it's further compounded by the fact that you weren't even going to be waiting.
Spence:	Why didn't you just call my cell?
Leo:	From what? A pay phone? *Laughs.* Actually, my friend here wanted to meet you. Alice, this is Spence. Spence, Alice.
Spence:	*Shakes her hand.* Hello Alice.
Alice:	Mr. . . . Spence.
Spence:	*To Sheila.* You must be Claire.
Sheila:	Uh . . . No. I'm Sheila.

Spence: Sheila, this is Leo, my brother-in-law . . . and his friend Alice . . .

Sheila: Hi Alice. Leo . . . You're the music lover.

Leo: Uh . . . sure.

Sheila: Spence was mentioning . . . that you listen to a lot . . . of music.

Leo: Was he?

Spence: Well you do.

Leo: So you were talking about me and you still forgot I was coming?

Spence: Evidently.

Alice: That's ironic too. Right?

Leo: Yes it is, and so I should be satisfied. But I'm not. I'm provoked. Provoked to ask . . . Where were you going?

Spence: Uh . . .

Sheila: We hadn't really decided.

Leo: Interesting. Are you old friends?

Sheila: No. As a matter of fact—

Spence: Hey! Leo, we need to talk for a moment. Excuse us ladies.

Leo: I'm not a lady.

Spence propels Leo a few feet away. The women are mildly uncomfortable, yet also slightly amused.

Spence: So . . . what are you gunning for here?

Leo: I don't know. Information?

Spence:	Well there's not a lot to be had. I just met Sheila at the chiropractor's. We had an interesting conversation. It was . . . unusual. And we wanted to talk a little more. So we're off to do that. I'm sorry I forgot about you, but—
Leo:	*Looks at the CD Spence is holding.* Hey! What's this . . . *Takes it.* "Gurrelieder?" What are you doing with this?
Spence:	It's Sheila's. She was letting me listen to it. It was kind of what we connected over.
Leo:	"Gurrelieder?" She ensnared you with Schoenberg?
Spence:	She didn't . . . It wasn't—
Leo:	Okay, listen. Everything has just completely changed. I was skeptical, but now I'm fascinated. I can't wait to see where this goes.
Spence:	Alright great, but that doesn't mean you're going to stick around.
Leo:	Welllll . . .

Alice and Sheila have started chatting quietly. Sheila exclaims abruptly.

Sheila:	What? Oh my God!
Spence:	*Turns.* What's going on?
Sheila:	Alice, that's amazing! What a day for you! *To Spence.* Alice was just telling me that she almost died today. She was choking on a little bone from a sandwich and Leo saved her.
Spence:	You did?
Leo:	So it seems.
Spence:	Did you do the Heimlich?
Leo:	It was a variation.

Spence:	Well that's great. Congratulations.
Sheila:	Yes, congratulations to both of you. *To Spence.* Apparently, they've just been celebrating ever since.
Spence:	And so you should. *Poking Leo.* You . . . You saved a life.
Sheila:	So Alice . . . do you think it changed you?
Alice:	I think it has. Everything's been kind of exciting. Simple things are so enjoyable.
Sheila:	Shopping would be a riot in this frame of mind.
Alice:	I guess it would. But I can't really go wild that way.
Leo:	The bonus she got was time, not cash.
Sheila:	But you could try stuff on.
Leo:	Yeah, really expensive stuff.
Sheila:	Exactly. Okay look, I have a store near here. I own it. We sell great clothes. High-end stuff. Alice, you wanna try on some gowns?
Alice:	Well yeah!
Sheila:	Is that good?
Spence:	You sell gowns? Like big . . . gowns?
Sheila:	Yeah. *Gestures expansively.* Fairly big. So . . . should we go do that?
Leo:	I sure think so. Spence?
Spence:	*Convincing himself.* Yeah. If that's what everyone wants to do. This is Alice's day. It has to be. Yeah.
Sheila:	Well perfect. Follow me to the gowns. *She leads them off.*

Scene Nine

At Sheila's dress shop, a little later. Spence stands by a display table with some magazines and a large floral arrangement. He's flipping through a magazine. The CDs and player are on the table beside him. Leo enters with a champagne bottle and glasses.

Leo: Hey, guess who's got champagne! Me!

Spence: Well that's great? Are we nearly done here?

Leo: God no. They've just started trying things on.

Spence: Both of them?

Leo: Oh yeah. It's a festival. *Filling glasses.* This is a fine store.

Spence: Is it? Why's that?

Leo: Well, because everything's expensive.

Spence: That's all?

Leo: No, the gowns are really humongous too. You could spend a lot of dollars here, but you'd be leaving with a lot of fabric, and that doesn't always happen.

Spence: Smells like a bargain.

Leo: Spence, I think you should buy Alice a dress.

Spence: What?

Leo: Come on, you can afford it. It would cap the day really nicely for her.

Spence: I don't doubt that. But I may have to go into a deposition with Carol next week. I have to account for everything I make and everything I spend. I don't want to have be explaining receipts for random gown purchases for women I just met.

Leo: Right, okay. That's a good grown-up reason and I won't push the matter. *Hands Spence a glass.* Here.

Spence: Thanks. *Holds out a magazine.* What do you think about these jodhpurs?

Leo: They're alright. They seem to fit her.

Spence: Not hers. The ones the man is wearing. What do you think?

Leo: What do you mean what do I think? Are you planning to get a pair?

Spence: I've never worn anything like that. They're kinda dashing, aren't they? They'd be a different look for me.

Leo: Maybe, but . . . *Gripping Spence's arm* . . . don't. Just don't.

Spence: But they look great with— . . . You're just being negative because I won't buy your friend a dress.

Leo: That's not true. You asked me my opinion and I gave it to you.

Spence: But with no reason attached.

Leo: *Laughs.* You don't need a reason not to wear jodhpurs. *Becomes serious.* Just don't.

Spence: Okay, whatever.

Leo: I think we need to talk a little business while the ladies are occupied.

Spence: Do we? Okay.

Leo: It's the reason I didn't write those five pages of the script.

Spence: The opening?

Leo: Yeah. It wasn't just because I was distracted by Alice.

Spence:	Really? So there were lots of other good reasons?
Leo:	No, just one important one. I found out that the thing at the end . . . The bit with the nun . . . It's been done.
Spence:	Really?
Leo:	Yeah, in some old movie . . . *I Married the Sea Hag* . . . something like that.
Spence:	So . . . you have to change the ending, and therefore you couldn't start.
Leo:	The ending was the part I liked.
Spence:	Well then maybe you really need to come up with a whole other idea. Something just completely different. It's obvious the angle we've been taking isn't really working for you and—
Leo:	But I'm just trying to do what you want.
Spence:	Okay, well I think I want something different now. *Picks up the CD case.* Something more like this.
Leo:	A medieval epic?
Spence:	Not necessarily. Just a really simple love story between two people but where the feelings are just gargantuan. I think I was completely on the wrong track. I said I wanted something different from what I get to do on my show. It's all about love and romance and seduction, but it's never even slightly overwhelming. I want people to feel like I did when I started listening to this.
Leo:	Which was how?
Spence:	Overwhelmed.
Leo:	That's so general.
Spence:	No, it's not. I was overwhelmed because I understood

what the two people . . . What the king and the girl . . .
were experiencing.

Leo: I'm amazed by this. I'm amazed that you would just listen to something like this once and have this reaction.

Spence: Yeah, well, who knew all you had to do was pay attention?

Leo: So . . . did you cry?

Spence: No.

Leo: You're sure?

Spence: No. I mean yes.

Leo: Uh-huh . . .

Spence: Sheila said . . . She said my eyes were shiny.

Leo: Oh God!

Spence: Well what . . . I was moved. I'm not ashamed of that. I—

Leo: No, it's not that. It's . . . The vengeful queen holding the
torch on the battlements . . . *Finds a page in the CD booklet.* "Her eyes glittered with the tears she did not wish to
shed."

Spence: Wow! I didn't get to that part.

Leo: This Sheila seems to be a very important person.

Spence: I'm glad you think so. You know, I washed her car once.

Leo: But I thought . . . Oh . . . *Laughs* . . . Right. You know that
the girl dies? Tovelille is poisoned by King Waldemar's
wife and so he goes mad and curses God and is condemned to ride every night with the armies of the dead.

Spence: Oo.

Leo: We can downplay that part. I usually bail before then anyway, even though it's fraught with musical interest. *Looks
at the* CD. I haven't heard this version. It's pretty new.

Spence: *Offers the player.* Here, have a listen.

Leo: Mmm . . . A machine like that's a bit candy-ass for this
particular work. I'm going to put it on the store system.

Spence: Might be a bit much for people shopping.

Leo: There are no people. I think we're closed.

Spence: Oh. Fine then.

Leo: It'd be a bit much for you? Is that what you're saying?

Spence: No. Put it on.

Leo: Yay.

*He exits. Spence looks around a bit, faintly puzzled by just about every-
thing. He picks up the magazine and resumes flipping through it. After a
moment one of the "Gurrelieder" orchestral interludes is heard. It's rela-
tively gentle and glowing and Spence puts down the magazine and listens.
As the music builds a little he contemplates the vase of flowers and after a
moment, he pulls out a rose. He breathes in its scent, then impulsively yet
softly kisses it. The music cuts off abruptly.*

Spence: Hey! Why'd you turn that off?

Leo: *Offstage.* It's not the part I wanted to hear.

*Spence rolls his eyes and puts the flower back in the vase. The music comes
on again, much louder. This time it's the full orchestra hammering away
at phrases which are almost, but not quite, discordant. Leo enters.*

Leo: *Very loudly.* Isn't this great!

Spence: *Also shouting.* What's happening now?

Leo: All's not well in the kingdom!

Spence: This part's harder to take!

Leo: WELL SCHOENBERG'S NOT GOING TO BE DENIED HIS STATUS AS A SERIALIST!!

Spence: AS A WHAT?

Leo: A SERIALIST!!

Spence: YEAH, YOU CAN TELL THAT IT'S SERIOUS!!

Leo: ISN'T THIS GREAT? THIS IS SO GREAT! IT'S SO LOUD!!!

As the music reaches the peak of its volume they stop yelling and stand back to back, a little frightened by the sheer weight of sound. As the music changes to a much broader and romantic phrase Alice and Sheila enter, both stunning in Oscar-worthy gowns. They move in a circle around the men who stare at them slack-jawed in wonder. The music becomes softer, yet no one speaks. Spence takes two flowers from the vase and gives one to each lady. They stand and stare at one another, smiling, and swaying a little. The music grows insistent once again and Sheila exits. After a moment, the sound switches off abruptly. Leo, Spence, and Alice turn away from one another, mildly embarrassed. Sheila returns.

Sheila: Sorry everybody. I have neighbours. There's a Christian Science Reading Room upstairs . . .

Spence: Mm-hm, mm-hm. Of course.

Leo: I'd like to say that . . . both of you . . .

Alice: Yes?

Leo: Well you look just lovely. Uhhh . . . I wanted to do better than that. But maybe I don't have to. It's not about what I think, it's about what you are.

Spence: Which is lovely.

Alice and Sheila: Thank you.

Leo: It's absurd how lovely you are!

Alice: Yes! That's what I'm feeling! Absurdly lovely! Look at me!
          Look at her! Look at me! I'm in Santa Monica in Versace,
          okay I know it's a knock-off, but the thing is that it just fit.
          It just went right on. Right on!

Leo: Right on!

Alice: That doesn't happen to me. *Smacks Leo in the chest.* That
          wouldn't even have happened to me in heaven! *Squeezes
          Leo's arms.* You! You! I squeeeeeeze you! I lick you!

She licks his face. He giggles.

Alice: I'm completely out of control. Am I drunkest at the party?

Sheila: I don't think so. It's just the dress.

Spence: You should be making a speech in that. You should be
          onstage accepting an award.

Alice: Oh for what though? I didn't do anything, really.

Leo: Still . . .

He turns to the others and they consult for two seconds. Leo turns back.

Leo: Alice, word just came in! You've been selected Best Lady!

Alice gasps and covers her face with her hands as the others applaud.

Leo: Speak! Speak!

All: Speak, speak!

Alice moves to the centre of the room. The others sit at her feet.

Alice: Thank you. Thank you one and all. I cannot tell you what
          it means to have been chosen Best Lady on this day of all
          days. Truly, I'm all choked up. Ah-ha-ha! There's a lump
          in my throat. Haaa—. . . ! Oh, I had some notes written

down but I guess I forgot them. I just didn't think I'd win. I've never won anything before. I did get a really nice review in the newspaper when I played Irene Molloy in *The Matchmaker* in Tacoma. But I didn't have to thank anyone. I just had to buy the paper. Okay now, I really have to focus a bit . . .

She breathes in and out a couple of times.

I wish there was music again. That made it easier to live up to the dress. Although I guess when the orchestra plays that means it's time to to wrap up. So anytime you want to hit it there Maestro . . . *Pause.* This is kind of a nightmare. I'll bet it's the worst Best Lady speech ever.

Leo: No!

Spence: No!

Sheila: We love you Lady!

Alice: Thanks. Thanks everyone. You know, I really have been grateful and wonderstruck for most of the day now, and I think that's getting a bit tired. So I guess I'll just make this an acceptance speech in the most basic way I can think of. I accept this honour gladly and I accept the extra time I've been given even more gladly, and I do mean both for my remaining existence and for this speech. Listen . . . Life is valuable. If it ends, you'd miss it. Remember that, but also forget about it. I'm done. Where's my drink?

All: *Applauding.* Brava! Hooray for Best Lady!

Leo: *Gives Alice a glass of champagne.* Well done. You'll be quoted.

Alice: My friend Sheila here has a great outfit too. I think she deserves to be heard.

Sheila: Oh! Oh, well . . . Yes, alright. If I was only going to thank one person, it'd have to be the guy I met in Tower Records last week, the one who said "Try a little Schoenberg. It's a left turn worth making." Whoever you were sir, wherever you are . . . You're a smartie and I salute ya!

All: Hear hear! Hurrah stranger! (etc.)

Sheila: Anyone else? Anyone care for the floor? Gentlemen?

Leo: We're not really dressed for it.

Spence: Actually . . . actually I wouldn't mind. I wouldn't mind saying something. *Moves to centre.* I guess . . . The thing is . . . I've been playing dramatic scenes for years on TV, and I've been married, and I've cheated on my wife and . . . *Laughs.* Well I've never said that out loud before. Sorry. So anyway, I've had those experiences and . . . I just . . . *Pause.* No . . . It's gone. I've lost the thing I was going to say about that. Sorry. Sorry everyone.

He moves off, then stops abruptly.

Spence: I'm not lost though. I don't feel lost, and usually I do.

Leo: Maybe that's what you were going to say?

Spence: I don't think so. I was really going to go on about something. Strange . . .

Sheila: Leo, anything from you?

Leo: Sure, I don't mind. No insight though, just trivia. I'll bet none of you knew that Arnold Schoenberg actually spent the last two decades of his life right here in Los Angeles. After composing "Gurrelieder," "Verklaerte Nacht," and other Late Romantic milestones, and subsequently spearheading the New Viennese School of twelve-tone composition that was the logical outgrowth of the late-nineteenth century vogue for chromaticism, Schoenberg moved to Brentwood and bought a bungalow.

Sheila: Remarkable!

Alice: Who'd have thought!

Spence: Leo is always brimming with interesting yet useless information.

Leo: Ah, but I don't think it is useless. What I'm telling you is that it'd be completely possible for you to take that CD that you like and a little player and go and listen to it on Schoenberg's lawn.

Spence: Oh! Yeah! Jesus, that'd be amazing . . . What . . . synchronicity?

Leo: Sure, or . . . a different word . . . A real one.

Alice: So should we go there? Should we go to Schoenberg's house?

Leo: I don't think we can. I don't really know the address. We should go somewhere though.

Sheila: I agree. For 'tis but the shank of the evening.

Spence: Yes, and that's when . . . wait, wait . . . when the scudding clouds gather close against the margin of the sky.

Sheila: Yeah!

Alice: *To Leo, indicating Spence.* This guy's just all over the map. I love it.

Leo: I know. He's interesting today. Capacious.

Alice: Mmm.

Spence: We were going to go for margaritas. I remember that now.

Sheila: Perfect. Let's find a view. The ocean, the sunset . . .

Alice: We should probably change.

Leo: No, don't!

Alice: But—

Spence: He's right. You can't just not look like this anymore.

Leo: Not when you're Best Lady.

Spence: No changing. We won't allow it.

Alice: I think that's maybe up to Sheila, since—

Spence: Nope. No, it isn't. *Takes out his wallet.* I'm buying this gown for you right now!

Leo: Hooray!

Alice: Oh no, I . . . When would I ever wear this again?

Leo: Who cares? Remember your own words . . . Acceptance . . .

Alice: You're right. *Importantly.* I accept the dress.

Spence: Perfect. *Hands Sheila a credit card and gestures to her dress.* And of course . . .

Sheila: You know technically, I kind of already own it.

Spence: Right. *Inaudibly, to Leo.* Whew!

Sheila: But thank you! *She gives him a peck on the cheek.*

Alice: Yes! Thank you Spence! *She gives him a kiss also.* I'll just get this rung in and and we can go. You fellas aren't going to feel underdressed?

Leo shrugs.

Spence: Compared to other circumstances I've been in, not really.

Sheila laughs and exits, followed by Spence. Alice looks puzzled and Leo murmurs and gestures as they go.

Scene Ten

Sheila is seated on a patio with a view of the ocean. She has Spence's sunglasses on. Leo enters with a tray of drinks in amusing cactus shaped glasses.

Leo: Oh, a woman. Mysterious and alone.

Sheila: I am those things, but you do know me . . . a little. *Lowers the glasses.* It's Sheila.

Leo: Aha! Where are the others?

Sheila: They went across the street to that big drugstore to get more sunglasses.

Leo: A good idea. *Squints into the sun.* The orb of day shines brightly, even as it lowers itself into the watery . . . waters. *Sets down the tray and putting on his own sunglasses.* Those are Spence's you're wearing?

Sheila: They are.

Leo: They look good. Don't give them back. Look, margaritas. And they're real.

Sheila: As opposed to . . .

Leo: The slushy pretend kind. Or are those what you prefer?

Sheila: Hell no. Okay, sometimes. But a novelty glass makes everything just fine.

Leo: Doesn't it. I insisted on these. *Gives her one.* Here. Cheers.

They tap the glasses together with a disappointing click.

Leo: Ting!

Sheila: Ting!

They drink. There's a pause.

Sheila: You're being very generous with me Leo.

Leo: What? What do you mean? I'm not paying and . . . you're like the hostess of everything.

Sheila: Sure, but I just think . . . maybe this isn't easy for you . . . given the circumstances of your relationship with Spence and his with me, whatever that actually is and—

Leo: You mean because he's still married to my sister?

Sheila: Yes. That.

Leo: Well the thing is . . . I love Carol a whole lot and she's really tried to do a ton for me, but Spence is pretty great too, especially today, and the worst thing about either of them is that they're married to each other and they shouldn't be. They were victims of circumstance.

Sheila: How so?

Leo: He was shooting a movie-of-the-week in Vancouver and she was a makeup artist on it and the thing about your nation's strong currency is that Canadian brides can be really inexpensive to woo. The wining, dining, and gifts budget just doesn't seem to run out, so there's all this delirious excitement on both sides that just builds and builds, but the bottom line is, everyone knows it's really false economy to buy things just because they're on sale. *Pause.* That sounds crass, but I was at the wedding and I could tell that they didn't like each other, at least not as much as they liked a lot of the other people who were there. You don't need to know any of this though. He likes you a lot.

Sheila: I feel like we've hardly spoken.

Leo: Is that a surprise really? On your first date you've been competing for attention with two other people and a massive classical concert work.

Sheila: Those are blessings though. If it'd just been the two of us, it probably would have felt awkward and though we might have been able to resolve that in a really exciting way, we likely would have regretted it. Presently, I have no regrets.

Leo: You'll get to stroll on the beach with him later. I'm certain of it.

Sheila: That'll be nice.

Leo: And if you can maybe prevent him from walking into the ocean because it would be a beautiful act, well I'd appreciate that.

Sheila: I can only try.

Leo: Good. *Clinks her glass.* Ting.

Sheila: Ting.

They drink. There's a little pause.

Sheila: One question though.

Leo: Yes?

Sheila: Who's Claire?

Leo: Ahh. To know that, I'm afraid you must . . . tune in tomorrow.

Spence and Alice enter with several pairs of sunglasses and a shopping bag with a medium sized box in it.

Spence: Here we are. Glasses all round.

Leo: *Lifts his glass.* Here too.

Alice: We bought more than we needed. Just couldn't decide.

Sheila: What else did you get?

Alice: *Holds up the box.* A blender!

Spence: Seven speeds for $27.95. Four bucks a speed. Couldn't pass that up.

| **Alice:** | I'm paying him back for it though. Enough's enough. |

| **Leo:** | No! You're wrong. |
| **Alice:** | I'm not. |

| **Leo:** | Okay, enough's enough, but that's all it is. Let's see those glasses. |

Spence puts the glasses on the table.

| **Sheila:** | Oh, I like those. |

She takes off Spence's and tries on a pair. Alice also puts on a pair and Spence puts his own on.

| **Sheila:** | Leo, what do you think? |

| **Leo:** | I don't know. Maybe switch. |

The women switch.

| **Leo:** | Mmm. Alice switch with Spence. |

They do.

| **Leo:** | Okay, Sheila, let me try yours. |

They exchange.

| **Leo:** | Now Alice, switch with me, and Sheila and Spence, you trade. |

They do.

| **Leo:** | Yes? |

Everyone murmurs happily.

| **Leo:** | Now let's see how they work. |

They all turn to face the sun.

All:	Ahhhhh.
Leo:	Now look, here are serious drinks in whimsical vessels.
Spence:	What's with this? Have they melted?
Leo:	No, they're just not the slushy kind.
Spence:	Right. Of course. These are real and they are better.
Leo:	And we get to keep the glasses.
Spence:	Would you use them again?
Leo:	Probably not. But they're good clutter.
Alice:	I'll be wanting one as a souvenir, in case I don't see any of you again.
Sheila:	Alice, why would that happen?
Alice:	Well . . . aren't we all strangers?
Spence:	I don't think we are.
Leo:	Mmm . . . No, Alice has a point. Even you and I, Spence . . . It's not like we really even . . .
Spence:	What?
Leo:	I'm sorry. I just got tired of what I was about to say before I even said it. Alice's observation is not insignificant, but we have better things to do than debate its merit.
Sheila:	Like getting her phone number for example.
Leo:	Exactly. *Raises his glass.* I say simply . . . Should old acquaintance be forgot . . . we'll be fine!
All:	Hear hear.

They click their glasses together and drink. They turn and look at the sun again.

Spence: There aren't any clouds today.

Alice: It's unusual. It's beautiful.

Spence: I was kind of primed to see some.

Alice: Right, you said something about that. I didn't understand that.

Spence: I wanted to see them scudding . . . hurrying . . . *Points.* Thattaway.

Sheila: On toward the margin of the sky.

Alice: The horizon?

Sheila: I think it's the same thing. *To Leo.* Isn't it?

Leo: If you like.

Sheila: Well isn't it? I'm asking you because you're verbally astute.

Leo: But your question involves nouns.

Sheila: Heh? Oh. You're teasing my mind.

Spence: *Gets up and moves forward.* I think Sheila's right. The margin is the horizon. It's the line that separates the sky and the water.

Alice: *Also gets up, joins Spence.* Why not just call it that then? It's the horizon. People know what that is.

Sheila: *Joins them.* There has to be a bigger point. It's a deliberate choice of phrase. It must mean something.

They turn and look at Leo.

Leo: Oh. I have to say?

Spence: You should contribute. We know you can.

Leo: *Gets up with some reluctance.* I don't know how worked up we need to be about this. The phrase is a line from a translation. It may not reflect the original author's intent at all.

Sheila: But we've been struck by it just the same.

Leo: Fair enough. Maybe it's the weight of the words. It's an aggregation of syllables that fall gratefully from then tongue because they're stressed at dependable intervals. The MAR gin OF the SKY.

They stare at him.

Leo: No? Okay, maybe it's an evocation of Melville. It's *Moby Dick*. It's in there somewhere. The spray . . . the spray from the white whale's leap . . . is seen against the blue plain of the sea and the bluer margin of the sky . . . the still blue plain . . . the still bluer margin . . .

Spence: Why do you just know that?

Leo: Because I read the book? *Pause.* Are we thinking I'm a little weird?

Spence: No one said that. The idea seems to have occurred to you.

Sheila: I'm not satisfied. I don't think the clouds are scudding toward the margin of the sky as a tribute to Melville.

Leo: No, you're probably correct.

Alice: Maybe it's the unimportant part of the sky.

Leo: What?

Alice: It's marginal.

Sheila: Oh. Interesting . . .

Spence: That makes sense to me. It's just that little bit over there in the extreme distance that you can hardly see. *Gestures.*

| | All this . . . above us . . . This is the better part. It's the big expanse of blue that's all around us. |

Leo: So the margin . . . is marginal? That's it?

Spence: Yes.

Sheila: Why do you think the clouds go there?

Leo: I don't know. Ask a meteorologist.

Alice: I don't think he likes our answer.

Spence: Leo?

Leo shrugs.

Spence: Well let's have it then. Tell us why we're wrong.

Alice: It won't hurt our feelings.

Leo: I can't. I can't tell you because I don't know. I don't know what you want to know and I don't know why I'm supposed to know it.

Sheila: Do you need time to think?

Leo: That can be helpful.

Spence: Not always though.

Leo: Hey! What's that mean?

Spence: Well just . . . That's your thing. Thinking and thinking and thinking . . . It's what you like to do, you don't seem to get tired of it, but I'm not sure it gets you anywhere. You don't write anything down.

Leo: I don't want to talk about this.

Spence: I'm not saying I do. It was an observation.

Leo: Yes . . . one that may have wrecked the party.

There is tense pause.

Alice: No. It didn't. That couldn't happen.

She gives him a little kiss.

Sheila: Alice is correct. *Kisses him also.* But we're going to excuse ourselves for a moment.

Leo: Okay.

The women exit.

Leo: Alice is correct. So I'm wrong now. How did that happen so fast.

Spence: Irony works quickly.

Leo: Hey! That was sharp. Good for you.

Spence: You think I want you to answer big questions and I don't. That's what you want to do. I need you to lay out a little story for me. That's all. I shouldn't have suggested that it be anything in particular.

Leo: Specifics are helpful. They anchor the imagination.

Spence: Unless they're dumb.

Leo: So what then?

Spence: Just make it how you want it. Write down what you know.

Leo: The truth as I've observed it?

Spence: That sounds good.

Leo: Truth is stupid.

Spence: You think?

Leo: Truth is such a rare thing, it is delightful to tell it.

Spence: You're quoting someone.

Leo: Emily Dickinson.

Spence: She's got a good rep.

Leo: Sure. She told the truth as she saw it, and that's how everyone knows that she was damaged goods, irreparably tainted by a life of quiet desperation.

Spence: Well then don't do it like her. Leave yourself out of it. Just tell the truth about others.

Leo looks at Spence incredulously.

Spence: That'd be fun, wouldn't it?

He smiles and exits. Leo thinks for a moment.

Leo: No! That's the worst thing I could possibly do.

Scene Eleven

As the peculiar little woodwind introduction to "Gurrelieder's" 'Song of the Wood Dove' is heard, Leo crosses to the park bench where he first met Alice. She's sitting eating her sandwich as before, and he bends over to check his shoe. After a moment, she starts to choke. He notices and reaches awkwardly to help her. As soon as he touches her, she coughs and pulls away from him.

Alice: It's okay. It's okay. I'm alright.

Leo: Well good. I thought you were—

She coughs. Leo holds out his water bottle.

Leo: Do you need a drink of something?

Alice: *Clears her throat.* No, it's fine. I'm fine. *Coughs.* There's a water fountain just there. *She starts gathering up her things, still rasping a bit.*

Leo: I don't mind if you—

Alice: I'm fine! *She starts to go, then turns.* Thanks though.

Leo: Sure.

She exits. He sits and stares after her for a moment. Jaunty classical music, probably Vivaldi, is heard, and Leo crosses to another part of the stage where he picks up a CD off a table and studies it. Sheila approaches carrying a couple of CD s.

Sheila: Excuse me, do you work here?

Leo: Who, me? No.

Sheila: Oh, I'm sorry. I just thought . . . I don't know why but I thought—

Leo: I do know some things. If you have a musical question I might still be able to help.

Sheila: Oh, well. I was just looking at this set here . . .

Leo: Uh-huh, "Gurrelieder." It's great.

Sheila: Is it? I was just noticing the price and it's practically two for one. You can't beat that, and I thought . . . something new and different . . . maybe . . .

Leo: It is different. It's an unusual work. But I'd say it's a left turn worth making.

Sheila: I'm not sure what you mean.

Leo: Do you know Schoenberg's music?

Sheila: I don't think I do. I've heard Schubert. And Schumann. I liked them.

Leo: Schoenberg can get a little cranky. But this is early for him and he mostly doesn't. It's very passionate. It's a medieval love story with a big Late Romantic sort of score. Very large orchestra. Big singing. That's not a problem?

Sheila: Oh no. I noticed this has Jessye Norman with the Boston Symphony. I saw her on PBS with the Boston Pops and I certainly enjoyed that.

Leo: Yeah, this is a little different. But good. It's still luscious.

Sheila: And there's another singer . . . Tat . . . tattit . . .tan . . .

Leo: Tatiana Troyanos.

Sheila: Right. She might want to trim that down a bit.

Leo: She can't at this point. She died.

Sheila: Oh.

Leo: In 1993. August the 21st.

Pause.

Sheila: Were you close?

Leo: No. I just . . . really loved her voice. It was . . . plangent.

Sheila: Well, this probably is as interesting as you say and it might be good for me to hear it someday, but really, I kind of want things I can play in my store and this probably wouldn't quite fit the bill. I think I'll just get this Andrea Bocelli here. Him I already know I like, and it's a Best of . . . Yeah, that's what I'm going to do. Thanks though. It was nice talkin' to ya.

She looks around for a moment, holding out the "Gurrelieder" set. He takes it from her. She smiles and exits.

Leo: But . . . Troyanos . . .

The plangent voice of Tatiana Troyanos is heard, singing the 'Wood Dove's Lament' from "Gurrelieder." Leo stands for a moment, then the lights cross fade as he moves over to his desk and sits in his chair. The music continues to play loudly as he sits looking a bit addled. Abruptly, he slides out of his chair and disappears behind the desk. Spence enters, talking loudly on a cell phone.*

Spence: Hang on! Hang on! I've just gotta fix this. *He picks the remote control off the desk, holds it out and presses a button. The music fades out.*
That's better. No kidding, not one of my picks. Yeah, no, I'm at my office. Well it's not mine, I don't work here. Like I'd need an office. I've been renting it for Carol's brother Leo. Right, yeah, I told you about that. He's supposed to be writing me a screenplay. Uh-huh . . . Mmmm. Nothin' so far. Lotsa talk, but not even an outline. I don't if know there's a problem . . . Well I guess there is actually because there's nothing doing. I mean, we talk and talk and then we just have to talk again. Yeah . . . Yeah . . . I don't why we're still pretending anything's gonna happen. I don't want to produce a movie. That was Carol's thing and . . . Jesus, when you think it through it's pretty clear, isn't it. Yeah. Could be time for a little announcement.

Leo has quietly gotten up and sat back in the chair.

Spence: I don't look forward to that particularly, but it can't be helped. Nice guy. Funny. But ya know . . . other than ironic perspective, I'm not sure what he's bringing to the party. *Laughs.* Yeah. Okay, uh-huh, five's still great. Or . . . let's just say four-thirty and I'll rent clubs. Yeah yeah. Okay, good. *He clicks off the phone and turns.* Ahhhh!

Leo: Good afternoon.

Spence: Did you . . . Why . . .

Leo: *Flatly.* Bean dip. I'm bringing bean dip.

Spence: Aw Leo . . . Jesus . . . Don't . . . You can't . . .

Leo: What? It's over. Fine.

Spence: I didn't really say that. I just said that it might be time to—

Leo: Hey! Do what you have to do.

Spence: Look, it's just awkward because of the divorce and you know that as well as I do. And then we meet and you're telling me you want to add nuns to an action movie. I just wanted to steal something and fire a big gun and outrun an explosion.

Leo: And I wanted something better for you.

Spence: Why?

Leo: I don't know. Like I said, it's fine. Your movie isn't the reason I get out of bed in the morning.

Spence: Well what is?

Pause.

Leo: You should go.

Spence: You're kickin' me out?

Leo: I'm asking you to leave.

Spence: You can't exactly do that. If you recall, this is office is paid for by—

Leo: Yeah, I know what's what, believe me. I just don't want to talk about it right now. Not with you.

Spence: Leo—

Leo picks up the remote control and presses a button. 'The Song of the Wood Dove' continues, only much louder.

Spence: Don't. Jesus! I'm not done!!

Leo turns the music louder.

Spence: Would you just . . . TURN THAT SHIT DOWN!!

Leo: NEVER!!

As the music reaches its natural climax, Leo turns it even louder. Spence throws up a hand dismissively and exits. Leo stands still in the final sung line of music, then sits during the same curious woodwind phrases that began the scene. He turns off the CD. He sits very still. He looks at his computer, then closes it. He picks up a notepad and paper and writes something. He thinks again, then looks at the pad. He holds it up, turning it from side to side, the shakes his head like he's just noticed something extremely obvious.

Leo: Ohhhhh.

He stands, still looking at the paper.

Scene Twelve
As Leo stands, the others return to the patio area and seat themselves. The women are back in their gowns. All look at Leo as if he were still in front of them.

Sheila: Leo, we're back now.

Spence: We've got more drinks.

Alice: Won't you join us?

Leo: *From the desk.* In a minute.

He tears out the page he's been looking at and crosses to the patio. When he gets to the front of the patio, he folds up the paper and puts it in his pocket.

Leo: I'm sorry for disappointing everyone earlier.

Alice: Leo, you didn't.

Leo: Well I'm sorry I couldn't answer the question. I wasn't ready then, but now I am. *He speaks very clearly and thoughtfully.*

A margin is an edge. And on a piece of paper, it's a line that marks an edge, but it really only has meaning because it denotes a point of entry. You put your pen where the margin tells you to and that's it . . . You're in. *He turns his attention toward the horizon.* So the margin of the sky would have to be the point of entry for everything above. That's why you can never say it's the least significant part, any more than you'd say the door is the least important part of a house. It can't be.

The others stand and join him slowly.

Leo: The sky is huge. You can't pick a place to get into it just by looking up. But if you look straight on . . . you can let yourself think that there really is a part of the sky that touches this same earth on which we're all standing. You can let yourself think that if you travelled the distance between here and there you would actually get to it. Now, experience tells us that it doesn't really work that way, but standing here right now, I can't see a reason why it's not possible, and I think I'm all the better for that.

The sun sinks down to the margin and it exits the sky. In time, it approaches the other margin and it gets back in. I want to do that too. I want to go to the beautiful place and enjoy the view and then come back. I think we all do. And right now, if we're willing to look into the distance, it should seem to us as if we can.

The others look into the distance. They remove their glasses. The sunset prelude of "Gurrelieder" is heard.

Leo: It's evening now. Darkness slips into the sky as the sun takes its final leave. On Gurre's battlements, the beautiful Tovelille kisses the last of her roses and watches for her shining Waldemar. Here, it's the fair Margarita who attends upon her friends. Don't make her wait.

Awakened from their little reverie, the others murmur happily and return to the table. Leo remains looking out for a moment, then joins them.

Fadeout

STEWART LEMOINE has been writing and directing for Teatro La Quindicina in Edmonton, Alberta since 1982 and is the author of over fifty plays including *Cocktails at Pam's, Evelyn Strange, The Glittering Heart,* and *The Vile Governess and Other Psychodramas.* His annual productions at the Edmonton Fringe Theatre Festival between 1982 and 2002 were consistent sell-outs. Since 1994, he and Teatro have been resident at Edmonton's Varscona Theatre, and his plays have been successfully mounted in many other Canadian centres, including Toronto, Montreal, Calgary, and Winnipeg.

He's also collaborated on a series of cabaret revues with actress/singer Sheri Somerville, including *Songs of Me* and *Around the World with Me.* Stewart has been a playwriting instructor for adults and children, and has created new works with acting students at the University of Alberta and Grant MacEwan Community College in Edmonton. At the Varscona Theatre he serves as producer of the nationally acclaimed improvised soap opera Die-Nasty and the indescribable Euro-style variety show *Oh Susanna.* A four-time winner of Edmonton's Elizabeth Sterling Haynes Award for his work with Teatro, Lemoine won Toronto's Dora Mavor Moore Award for *The Vile Governess and Other Psychodramas.* In May 2003, he was honored with the Queen's Golden Jubilee Medal by the Lieutenant Governor of Alberta, Lois Hole.

Playography

All These Heels 1982 (co-written with Phil Zyp)

The Unremembered Budapest 1984

Dinah's Wine Bar 1984 (musical–composer Gary Lloyd)

Chicks Akimbo 1985

Women in Bed 1985

My Miami Melody 1985 (musical–composers Gary Lloyd and R.J. Smart)

The Vile Governess & Other Psychodramas 1986

What Gives? 1986 (musical–composers Gary Lloyd and R.J. Smart)

Cocktails at Pam's 1986

Neck-Breaking Car-Hop 1987

Swiss Pajamas 1988

Hopscotch Holiday 1988 (musical–composers Gary Lloyd and R.J. Smart)

Damp Fury 1988

Teens in Togas 1989 (musical–composer Gary Lloyd)

When Girls Collide 1989

All Ears 1989

Planet of the Lost Swing Babes 1990 (musical–composer Gary Lloyd)

The Glittering Heart 1990

The Swift Hotel 1990

The Hothouse Prince 1991

The Jazz Mother 1991

A Night With Barbara 1991

The Spanish Abbess of Pilsen 1992

Two Tall, Too Thin 1992

The Argentine Picnic & Other Lemoine Vignettes 1992

Shockers Delight! 1993

The Book of Tobit 1993

The Delightful Garden of Saint Piquillo 1994

The Visitation of the Paragon 1994

Connie in Egypt 1994

The Noon Witch 1995

The River Princess and the Frozen Town 1995

Evelyn Strange 1995

Fall Down, Go Boom: A Skater's Tragedy 1996

Fatty Goes to College 1996

The Velvet Shock 1996

The Lake of the Heart 1997

Fatty's Big Show 1997

Ludicrous Pie 1997

Pith! 1997

Whiplash Weekend! 1997

The Subject of My Affections 1998

The Rules of Irene 1998

Tales of the Electress 1998 (co-written with Trevor Anderson)

Fever-Land 1999

Fatty Goes Wild 1999

Skirts on Fire 2000

Orlando Unhinged 2001

On the Banks of the Nut 2001

Eros and the Itchy Ant 2002 (musical sequence composed by Ryan Sigurdson)

The Exquisite Hour 2002

Vidalia 2002

Caribbean Muskrat 2003 (co-written with Josh Dean)

The Margin of the Sky 2003